Instant Period Costumes

How to Make Classic Costumes from Cast-off Clothing

Barb Rogers

MERIWETHER PUBLISHING LTD.
Colorado Springs, Colorado

Meriwether Publishing Ltd., Publisher
PO Box 7710
Colorado Springs, CO 80933-7710

Editor: Theodore O. Zapel
Editorial Assistants: Sue Trinko, Renée Congdon
Typesetting: Sue Trinko
Cover and book design: Janice Melvin
Interior illustrations: Janice Melvin
Interior photography: Barb Rogers

© Copyright MMI Meriwether Publishing Ltd.
Printed in the United States of America
First Edition

All rights reserved. No part of this publication may be reproduced, stored in a retrieval system, or transmitted in any form or by any means, electronic, mechanical, photocopying, recording or otherwise, without permission of the publishers.

Library of Congress Cataloging-in-Publication Data

Rogers, Barb, 1947-
 Instant period costumes : how to make classic costumes from cast-off clothing / by Barb Rogers.
 p. cm.
 ISBN 1-56608-070-3 (pbk.)
 1. Costume. 2. Used clothing industry. I. Title.

TT633.R66 2001

2001030071

2 3 4 5   02 03 04

Dedication

*To my dad, Charley Chaplin, Buffalo, Missouri,
for believing in me and never giving up. Of all the things
I inherited, I thank you most for my creativity.*

*And to the loving memory of my daughter,
Nikki Lynn ... my tiniest angel. Gone but not forgotten.*

Acknowledgments

A special "thank you" to all the people who helped make this project a reality. I couldn't have done it without you.

Tom and Jacqui McKibben, Mattoon, Illinois; Christopher Brown, Sun City, Arizona; Dimetrius Vonglis, Sun City, Arizona; Paulette Harris and Patricia Pulsifer, Yarnell, Arizona; Kathy Smith and the girls at Kinko's in Prescott, Arizona; Tammy and Margret at the post office in Yarnell, Arizona.

And, to all the people who put their used clothing in yard sales or take them to the thrift stores where I find my treasures, waiting to happen.

But most of all, a special thank you to my husband, Junior, who lives through it all. You have the patience of a saint, thank God.

Contents

Introduction

I love to make costumes. When I started, I had no background in sewing. I had no idea how to use a pattern. I didn't own a sewing machine. But, I loved to make costumes.

Like many mothers, I started out making costumes for my son for school plays and Halloween. We didn't have much money, so I usually had to make them out of things I had around the house or from odds and ends from thrift shops. One year, when my son was in the second grade, I made an entire set of armor from cardboard and tin foil. He won first place at his school.

As the years wore on, I worked many other jobs but continued to make costumes for extra money. In my jobs, I never experienced the satisfaction I felt when I completed a wonderful costume that made a child smile. I always knew it was what I wanted to do but had no idea how to make a living from it. Later in life when I got the opportunity to attend college, I opted for the practical studies rather than learning more about theatre and costuming.

Then one day I was in a position where I had a choice. When I was asked, "What would you do, if you could do whatever you wanted?" I didn't have to think about it. I said, "I'd make costumes. I love to make costumes."

My journey into the world of costuming was one of learning through doing. I opened my rental shop upstairs in a two-story brick building over two bars on the main street of our small town. A year after I went into business, my friends bought me a treadle sewing machine at an auction for fifty dollars. I still have that machine today. Up to that point, everything I made had to be completely sewn by hand. Working alone, making all the costumes and running the shop, I looked for easier, faster and cheaper ways to make costumes.

My third year in business, I joined the National Costumer's Association. I went to a convention where I could take classes to learn to be a better costumer. I recall sitting in one of my first classes and wondering why that person was putting herself through all that tedious work. I could accomplish the same thing in less time, with less effort and much more cheaply, without compromising the integrity of the costume. For years, as a member, I wondered why people put themselves through the patterns, the measuring, the pinning and the sewing of basic garments when they could go to a thrift shop and buy the same thing for a few dollars and save all that time and effort.

My shop grew, and I learned the fast and easy ways to design costumes without having to learn to be a seamstress. In my fifth year, I made the decision to do costumes for theatre. It was a challenge, but I found I could use the same methods, which came in handy when I had to do *The King and I* for a high school and only had a couple of weeks to complete the costumes. It was a wonderful production and everyone was happy with the costumes.

By my tenth year in business, I had fifteen rooms of costumes and was getting calls from other places for costumes. I shipped costumes as far as London, England. It was working. I was converting used clothes into costumes and people liked them, wanted them and were willing to pay money for them. I'd found a way to do what I loved and make a living at it.

Due to a serious health problem, I am no longer able to run my shop, but I continue to love making costumes. When I moved to a small mountain community in Arizona to begin a career as a writer, which was another dream, I decided to combine the two. They say to write about what you know. I know about conversion costuming.

There are only a few rules to conversion costuming. The first and most important rule is that you must put aside all your preconceived ideas about how to make a costume. The world of conversion costuming is miles away from fabrics, measuring, pinning, cutting and sewing. The most important tool you need is your imagination.

You will be using pictures rather than patterns. Once you have a clear picture in your mind, you are ready to begin your search through thrift shops, rummage sales and antique stores. You are looking for a garment with the potential to become the costume you desire. Pay close attention to the lines of the garment. Are you looking for a high waist or no waist at all? Where should the man's jacket flare out? How long should the jacket be? What kind of lapel is needed? Try to find something with a similar cut. The closer you get in the basic garment, the easier it will be to convert.

For me, shopping becomes an adventure not unlike hunting. I'm in search of my prey. The excitement builds as I approach a rack of clothing and see just the slightest edge of the perfectly colored fabric peeking out between other garments. My adrenaline level rises as I reach for it and discover that it will work. Excitement builds when I realize it is in my price range. My heart pounds as I purchase it and transport it home, wash it and prepare it for conversion.

That takes us to rule two. Never pay any more for a garment than you have to. I set a limit for myself on what I'll spend on certain things. Wedding dresses are something that I'm always looking for, but the most I will spend is thirty dollars. I can usually find them for about twenty if I shop around. Many of the dresses I use cost under ten dollars. After spending a few dollars converting them, I can rent them in my shop for thirty-five to forty dollars. "Is that fair to the customer?" you might ask. Remember, the customer is financing the hunt and my imagination, along with the completed costume.

Now that you have your garment washed and hung up, look at it … really look at it. You are the artist and the garment hanging in front of you is the blank canvas. See it completed in your mind before you begin the work. When you are ready, it's time to consider the third rule. Never sew if you don't have to. I work under the K.I.S.S. principle: Keep It Simple, Silly. If you need to raise the skirt on one side, do you go through the trouble of finding the correct color thread, threading the needle and stitching it, or do you glue it or pin it? You can probably guess what I would do. Why would I spend half an hour working on something that I can do just as well in a few seconds?

The fourth rule is have fun. The more you enjoy what you're doing, the better it will turn out. When you don't have to go through the tedious and boring process of making the basic garment, you can get to the fun part more quickly. It's like people who decorate cakes. The fun part is in the design, not making the cake. So, I'll attempt to teach you in this book how to put aside the boring and mundane part of costuming and go right to the exciting and creative part.

The last rule is that there are no rules. That is the wonderful thing about conversion costuming. You can do whatever works as long as it looks the way you want, fits comfortably and is washable. I have many costumes in the shop that have been washed over and over, worn time and again, and have lasted more than ten years. One good thing about this is that if a costume happens to get destroyed after the first wear, you haven't lost much money.

I would like to invite you into the wonderful work of conversion costuming, where we can all play dress-up. Remember when we were children playing in adult clothing from an old trunk or closet? This isn't that much different from that. Open yourself to the child within who still wants to play dress-up and let her out. Let her stick a purple feather in a red hat. Let her cut, glue, pin and tie until it looks the way she wants. Let her have fun and come up with those great creations made of fantasy and old clothes.

Materials

Glue Gun

A glue gun and glue are the most important tools you will need. With them, you will be able to place fabric where you want, embellish your garment without sewing and seal raw edges. A glue gun produces a versatile substance that dries quickly, is washable and is a great time-saver.

I've tried several types of glue guns over the years. When they first came out, they were all "hot" glue guns. When I was beginning to wonder if I had any fingerprints left, I found the Magic Melt® glue gun, which is a low-temperature gun that works just as well. It can still burn you, but it doesn't go through three layers of skin. It dries more quickly than the hot gun and is washable. You can purchase the Magic Melt® glue gun and glue through discount stores or fabric stores, or check the reference section for the adhesive company I buy through.

For myself, I buy my glue in ten-pound bags of ten-inch sticks. That way I don't spend all my time feeding the gun, and I always have plenty on hand. Anything in this book that is glued, you can be assured is glued with a Magic Melt® glue gun and clear glue.

The one drawback to using this type of glue is that you cannot wash the garment in anything but cold water and either hang it to dry or use your dryer on air fluff. No heat! The glue will let go.

If for some reason your glue does let go, it is a simple matter to repair it with more glue. This product is wonderful for any type of repair. Imagine a beautiful Southern belle who comes back with a cigarette burn in the skirt. I can glue a piece of fabric on the back and then cover the hole with a silk flower, a piece of jewelry, or fabric paint. If the hem's not right on a man's suit, I can turn the pants inside out, fold them over to hem and touch glue the hem in. Later, I can wash the pants in warm water and release the hem so that the pants might be worn by someone else. As you will see in this book, a glue gun is faster, easier and more time-saving than sewing.

Scissors

Scissors are the next important tool. You will need a good, sharp pair of fabric shears. Since you will be doing a great deal of cutting, you will want a clean cut. With dull scissors, the fabric tends to pull and ravel, causing you no end of frustration. If you cut well with good scissors the first time, there is no need to go back and trim edges. I keep a second pair of scissors for cutting other items, such as foam, trim, cardboard and hats. If you use your fabric shears for anything but fabric, it will ruin them.

Safety Pins

Safety pins are a tool I use. There is nothing wrong with using a safety pin in a costume as long as you use it safely. If I use a pin in a garment where it might be next to the skin, I pinch the head of the pin with a pair of pliers, shoot glue over it and cover it with a piece of fabric or foam. If it is used on an outer layer of a garment, I use glue over it and cover it with some sort of trim. Pins are great when you have to drape fabric around a dress and attach it at intervals. With pins, you can move it until it looks right before you actually set the glue. My rule of thumb: Never sew if a pin will work as well.

Needle and Thread

I do keep a needle and thread on hand, just in case something comes up that I absolutely have to sew. I have an old treadle sewing machine I use to make mop hats, sew in elastic and put in some of the larger hems. I keep a neutral-colored thread in the machine, with black thread on the stand-by for darker fabrics. There have been times when I didn't have the color thread needed, so I used what I had and colored over it with a black marker. Whatever works! Just be sure you use a permanent marker.

Dye

I use a lot of dye for costuming. Imagine going into a thrift store and finding just the right garment, but it's the wrong color. Not a problem if you can dye it. After my first couple of disasters, I paid attention to the very succinct directions. First you must wash the garment and remove it from your washer, leaving it wet. Start your machine on the longest, hottest cycle, and add your dye. Because of the newer fabrics, you may want to add a half-cup of salt before you add the dye. The salt will help the dye bleed into the fabric better. Put your garment in and let the agitation cycle go almost to the end. Stop the machine and start the cycle again. The longer you run it, the more brilliant your color will be. If you just want a hint of color, run it through once. For instance, if I want a pale grey I can use a bottle of black dye through one cycle and get the desired color. If you want to get creative, you can mix dyes to come up with some interesting shades. I do that a lot when I'm wanting to achieve odd colors for period costumes.

Fabric Paint

Fabric paint is a godsend. Rather than spending many hours doing hand beading, I can accomplish the same thing in a short time with drops of fabric paint. Now that they have so many shades and types of paint, design possibilities are endless. I would warn you to always wash your garment or fabric before you begin or the sizing will keep your paint from absorbing into the fabric. As you will see, I use a lot of fabric paint in my costumes for embellishment, glitter and even buttons. Buttons can be a problem from time to time. You can use the paint on an existing button or make your own right on the garment from the paint. Of course, it has to be a decorative button, not one in use. Fabric paint is also useful in sealing a raw edge. If you want to cut an open space in the bodice of a dress, do it and seal the edges with a fabric paint design. It works great. When I use heavy trim, such as rhinestones, I like to put intermittent drops of fabric paint to help secure it. Fabric paint can be used on hats, masks, and for making jewelry, beading, an embroidered look or extra glitz on an otherwise dull fabric.

Trim and Old Jewelry

Keep your eye out for all sorts of trim and old jewelry. As I shop through thrift shops, garage sales, antique stores and discount stores, I am always on the lookout for anything that can be used for trim and decorative purposes. After Christmas, I'm the person at the discount stores with my basket full of beads, garland and wired gold stars. After Halloween, you'll find me there buying everything I can use that is seventy percent off. I watch for old belts, ties and hats throughout the year and buy when I find them cheap so I will have them on hand. I wait until the discount and fabric stores bag up their loose silk flowers and sell them for a couple of dollars a bag. As long as I can glue it on and it's washable, I use it for trim.

To recap, if you have a glue gun and glue, a pair of scissors, pins, a needle and thread, some dye, fabric paint and trim, all you need is the garment and you are on your way to creating a wonderful costume.

Making the Costumes

If you are looking for an authentic period costume, you are looking in the wrong book. This book is about the illusion of authenticity. The costumes depicted are about a certain period look. They will work well for plays, parades and theme parties, but not for reenactments where you desire the right kind of fabric, sewing and buttons.

Research is the key to period costuming. Go to the library, bookstores or video stores and see what a person wore during the period you're interested in. Pay attention to the details. I'm a firm believer that if you take care of the small details, the big ones will take care of themselves. Costuming is in the details!

Remember that you are only interested in the illusion of authenticity. It doesn't have to be correct, but it must look like it is. For instance, you wouldn't go through all the trouble of making a wire hoop underskirt when you can buy a boned underskirt that will give you the same appearance but be lighter weight, easier to wear and give you the same look … would you?

Many period costumes can be achieved by layering dresses, gluing trousers to jackets and cutting off skirts and draping them around other garments. When you have a clear picture in your mind of the look you want, let the hunt begin. You are not interested in the type of fabric, except that it is washable in case you have to dye it. You can only dye light to dark. Don't expect to buy a red garment and dye it pink. It won't work. Keep that in mind as you seek out your garments. I love to find white dresses and suits that I can dye the color I desire.

Pay attention to the style of your garment. One of the big mistakes in conversion costuming is fighting the line of the garment. Go with the flow of the gown, suit or robe … don't fight it. It will show in the final results.

Now that you've researched, found your basic garments and they are the desired color, don't be afraid to cut. Change that neckline, cut that collar off, split the sides or whatever else it needs. Keep in mind that if you make a mess out of it, you haven't lost that much money. You can go back to the rummage sales, the thrift stores or your grandma's closet and find something else if need be. If you've followed my guide, how much money could you lose?

I will attempt to show you, in a simple fashion, how to achieve the look you desire for less than thirty dollars, in about a half an hour, not counting the time for dyeing. Most of the trim and accessories are easily accessible to anyone. Anything used that I think you can't find, I will tell you where it can be purchased in the reference section at the back of the book.

Keep in mind the K.I.S.S. principle and remember we are going for a look, an illusion of authenticity, not the real thing. Be creative, have fun and end up with a wonderful period costume you will be proud to wear.

Underskirting

What you use to pouf out the skirt of a costume can be as important as the gown itself. For the purpose of this book, we will be shooting for an authentic look that is also cool, comfortable, easy to make and inexpensive.

Petticoats can oftentimes be found in thrift shops that carry wedding dresses and prom dresses. If you can't locate one, keep in mind that you can use the skirt out of a full gown that will serve the same look. If the gown has a zippered back, merely cut the gown off at the waist, leaving the zipper down, and glue the edge of the waist under. If you're worried about the zipper coming undone, cut a shoestring in half, tack it to each side of the opening and tie securely.

During the Elizabethan period, women wore farthingale underskirts. When you think of a farthingale, think of Queen Elizabeth. Her dress poufs out all around her. Creating a farthingale might seem like a difficult procedure, but in fact it is relatively easy to do. If you have a skirt or pair of slacks with loops at the waistband, cut the waist off just below the loops. (You will use the waistband portion for the farthingale, and can save the rest of the garment for other projects.) Leave enough fabric to glue the bottom edge under. Run boning through the front and back loops, leaving it to stand out on the sides as far as you wish. To hook the boning to itself, use large safety pins, but be sure you pinch the heads closed. If you use the pins, you can adjust the boning by sliding it.

When building the costume over a cartwheel farthingale, keep in mind the weight of the fabric you use. Use the heavier fabric in the back and front where the gown lays flat, but use lighter-weight fabric on the sides where it needs to stand out.

If you happen to have an old hoop skirt from a prom or wedding dress, with a few minor adjustments, you can achieve the same look. Either bring the waist above the breasts and tie at the waist with a string, or if you would feel more secure, add a pair of thin suspenders to hold the underskirt up high enough. Run a piece of elastic between the legs or a piece on each side of the legs, pull tight and secure with pins. Believe me, it will stick out on the sides.

To make a full circle French farthingale, do the same thing, omitting the piece of elastic between the legs or at the side of the legs. Instead, bring the bottom hoop up to the middle hoop and pin in several places.

Another way to do a full circle French farthingale is to make a bolster pillow that goes around the waist and ties in the front. This type would be hotter to wear because of the pillow filler but will accomplish the same look.

Hoop skirts can be a problem if you can't find one in a thrift shop. There is an easy way to make one inexpensively. Buy three pieces of PVC tubing at your hardware store, each one smaller than the other. Using an old belt that is thin and fits well at the waist, tape your smallest piece of tubing together and, with twill tape, fasten it to the belt in several places, leaving it to hang down as far as you want. Hook the second hoop to the first in the same way and then the third. If you are concerned about needing a bit of underskirt to show at the bottom of the dress, glue wide ruffled lace to the bottom hoop.

Bustles can be achieved by using many easy-to-find materials. I've made them from throw pillows, balled-up netting, a child's Nerf ball and even a plastic basket. Think simple where bustles are concerned. A piece of elastic for the waist that fastens in the front enables you to hook what you need on the back or sides for the look you desire. If you need your bustle to hang down farther in the back, merely attach whatever you're using to elastic or non-fray fabric that's the length you want.

In the 1880s, not only did the women wear bustles, but in many cases the entire back of the dress was full and needed to be held out from the body. That particular look can be accomplished by using a petticoat. Fold the petticoat in half at the waist and glue the two halves together. Attach it to a thin belt or piece of elastic so that it hangs down the back. Put your bustle on top of the petticoat. You will be surprised at the wonderfully authentic look it gives you.

During the 1950s and 1960s, women wore crinolines, more commonly known as can-cans. Believe me, you don't want to make a can-can. It's not a pleasant experience. I watch the rummage sale ads for sales that have square dance clothing. Many of the square dance can-cans are so full you can make two out of one. It's still pretty easy to find them in thrift shops too. However, if you can't find one, consider looking for a full-skirted cocktail dress or short prom dress with lots of skirting and netting under the outer skirt. If they're not the right color, you may be able to dye them. Cut them off at the waist, leave the zipper down, and glue the edge of the waist down just as you did for a petticoat.

Whatever type of underskirting you desire, think simply. It's going to be under the gown, away from prying eyes, so you can do whatever works and gives you that period look you want. Again, you must consider the weight of the fabric or dress used over the underskirting when you decide how to make it. If you choose to purchase underskirting, see the reference section at the back of this book.

Footwear

Many men's and women's period costumes require a pair of spats. This is not an easy thing to find in the thrift shops. In fact, I don't believe I've ever seen a pair there, so I came up with a simple solution. Socks! It was so simple that I didn't think it would work at first, but it gave me exactly the look I wanted.

Since you can buy socks in most colors, or buy white ones and dye them, the color range is huge. Once you have the color you wish, make sure you get a pair large enough to stretch over the shoes you're wearing. Put them over the shoes, cut the soles out and however much you need to cut off the top. Trim the edges off to give you the look you want and then glue the edges under. Attach pieces of elastic in two places, one near the front and the other so it goes under the shoe where the heel meets the sole. If you're wearing black shoes, use black elastic, etc. If you want the button look on your spats, glue on small buttons or make small buttons with fabric paint drops.

Under many of the crinoline and Elizabethan-style gowns, women can wear the little stretchy house shoes that are very inexpensive to buy new. They will be comfortable too.

For the Roman, Greek, Egyptian and Biblical costumes, sandals are suitable. If you need the kind that wind up the leg, use two shoestrings in the desired color, tie them to the sides of your sandals and crisscross them as you move up the leg. Tie them in the back. If you don't have shoestrings, use pieces of trim. Just be sure you don't use anything slick because the ties will slide down the legs before three steps have been taken.

During the time following World War II, white bucks for men and saddle oxfords (black and white shoes) for women became popular. It stands to reason if you can't find a pair of men's white shoes, you can paint a pair. If you want the two-tone brown and white, use a pair of brown shoes, tape off the part to stay brown, and spray paint the remainder white. You'll see ... they'll look great. For the saddle oxfords, use a pair of white tennis shoes, glue black fabric where you want the black, edge with black fabric paint to keep it from fraying, and you're ready for the hop.

Boots for pirates and cavaliers can be made like a pair of spats with a long top. Decide what color shoes you'll be wearing, buy any type of fake leather, cut a sock spat, lay it on the fabric and cut around it, leaving the top as long as you want. Use hook and loop tape at the back of the upper part to fasten it together and elastic underneath to secure it to the shoes. If you need pirate boots, leave enough at the top to fold over.

During the 1920s and 1930s, women wore pumps (high heels). Most of the heels today can work for the period. What you must be concerned with are the stockings. Ladies wore rolled-down hose during the 1920s and seamed hose during the late 1920s, 1930s, 1940s and even into the 1950s. If you can't find seamed hose, you can use a marker on a pair of pantyhose for the same look.

If you happen to purchase your footwear at a rummage sale, thrift shop or other place that handles used clothing, I would urge you to use a disinfectant on the inside of the shoes before you put your feet in them. Just like sharing stage make-up can transfer germs and rashes from one person to the next, so can feet fungi be transferred from one person to the next. In fact, one of the first things I do with anything I buy used is to clean it thoroughly.

If you want to know what type of shoes people wore during certain periods, go to the library, look at pictures of people from that era and then find a simple way to get the same look. Shoes can make or break a costume.

The
Costumes

Egyptian

Egyptian Man

Egyptian Man

When I think of the Egyptian man, I picture the Pharoah in the movie *The Ten Commandments*. His costumes were impressive. Although the common man wore very plain clothing and, in Egypt, were very scantily clad, the more wealthy wore richer fabrics, jewelry and wonderful headdresses.

I purchased a gold robe and an extra-large, blue velvet dress to create my Egyptian man.

Making the Costume

1. Robe: Remove the collar and turn the robe around backwards.

2. Cut out the large collar. Cut out the piece of fabric that hangs in the front of the costume.

3. Using glue, adorn the center of the collar and front flap with a rich material and trim with gold trim.

4. Velvet dress: Cut a slit up the center to the crotch and round off the corners. Glue the flap at the waist of the dress.

5. Glue gold trim around the hem and cuffs of the dress. Add a gold belt and necklace and sandals.

6. The headdress is made over a ball cap. Cut the bill off, glue the blue, rich material at the front and sides, leaving it hang down longer on the sides and shorter in the back. Glue wide gold trim at the front.

Robe

Velvet Dress

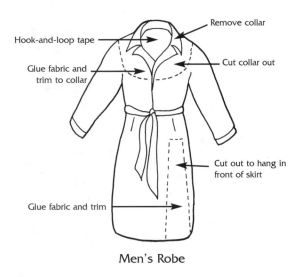

Remove collar

Hook-and-loop tape

Glue fabric and trim to collar

Cut collar out

Cut out to hang in front of skirt

Glue fabric and trim

Men's Robe

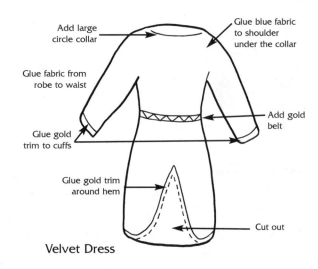

Add large circle collar

Glue blue fabric to shoulder under the collar

Glue fabric from robe to waist

Add gold belt

Glue gold trim to cuffs

Glue gold trim around hem

Cut out

Velvet Dress

T I P The rich blue fabric was purchased at a fabric store in the remnants section. There was enough left to make a drape over one arm that is glued to the shoulder of the dress, underneath the collar. The collar is hooked together in the back by a piece of hook and loop tape.

Egyptian Woman

Cleopatra was my inspiration for the Egyptian woman. Again, if you need costumes of the more common people of the period, you can use the same idea but toned down.

I found a turquoise robe that zips up the front and tied a string at the waist for the solid part of the costume and used a black, double-layer, sheer nightie to accentuate it. The collar and headdress were made from a heavy gold oilcloth-type fabric that was given to me. I had enough scraps to make armbands. The beading was from strands of an old plastic beaded curtain and drops of fabric paint.

Egyptian Woman

Making the Costume

1. Zip-up robe: Cut the bottom so that you leave a flap hanging down in front. Glue silver and black trim along the front zipper, and tie the tie in the back. The robe doesn't have to be hemmed because it is non-fray fabric. Glue plastic jewels and use fabric paint drops to decorate the skirt.

Sheer Nightie

Zip-up Robe

2. Cut the underdress of the nightie off under the arms and glue inside the waistline of the robe. With a safety pin, gather up the front of the nightie to the crotch. Glue a plastic jewel over the pin. Glue plastic jewels and use fabric paint drops to decorate the skirt.

3. Cut the collar out of the gold oilcloth, decorate with the same plastic jewels and fabric paints. Cut the outer nightie off under the arms and glue inside the collar for the drape.

4. The headdress is made from a wide, fabric-covered headband. Using cardboard that's covered with the gold oilcloth, glue it to the front of the headband so it will stand up, decorate it with the plastic jewels and fabric paint, and glue more of the jewels to the headband to hang over the hair. Add armbands fastened together with hook-and-loop tape.

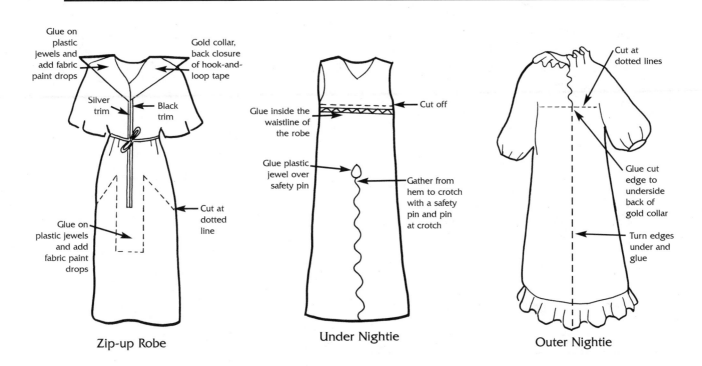

Glue on plastic jewels and add fabric paint drops

Gold collar, back closure of hook-and-loop tape

Silver trim

Black trim

Glue on plastic jewels and add fabric paint drops

Cut at dotted line

Zip-up Robe

Glue inside the waistline of the robe

Cut off

Glue plastic jewel over safety pin

Gather from hem to crotch with a safety pin and pin at crotch

Under Nightie

Cut at dotted lines

Glue cut edge to underside back of gold collar

Turn edges under and glue

Outer Nightie

Biblical

Biblical Man

Biblical Man

I located the heavy, white linen, extra-large dress at a thrift shop in Wickenburg, Arizona. When I got it home, washed it and put it on my mannequin, I knew I had a find. The only problem was deciding what costume to make of it. I ended up using it for several costumes in this book because it was so versatile. By snipping the elastic out of the inside of the waist, it hangs down far enough for a man's or woman's costume.

With the white dress as an underdress, I added an old blanket and white long-sleeved turtleneck to make the biblical man.

Making the Costume

1. White linen dress: Loosen the elastic from the inside waist. Press out.

2. Cut the neck and cuffs off a white turtleneck and use it under the dress.

3. Blanket: Lay it out flat. Bring the sides together to meet in the middle.

4. Use the white dress on top of the folded blanket for a pattern, folding the sleeves in. Cut the shoulders and armholes, as for a vest. Cut the blanket the length of the white dress. The folds are the sides.

5. Glue or sew shoulders for a hem. Round off or glue back the center for the look you desire.

6. Using what is left at the bottom of the blanket, cut a square and a long rectangle. Glue the square to the center of the rectangle, taking tucks.

7. Glue the top of the square together to make the hood.

8. Glue hood to the neck of the robe.

9. Add a tie belt and sandals.

Extra-large
Linen Dress

Robe Pattern

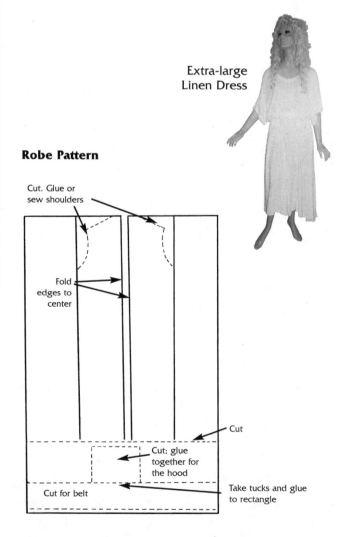

Biblical Woman

Biblical costumes seem to be relatively simple to make. As a rule, with very little changes you can use the layered look to achieve the desired look.

I used the heavy white linen dress with the elastic out of the waist for the underdress of the biblical woman. Because I wanted long sleeves, a white turtleneck with the cuffs and neck removed gave me the sleeves I needed and that wonderful layered look. There was no need to hem the neck or cuffs since the turtleneck was made of a non-fray T-shirt fabric, but I did use a little glue at the seams to keep them from pulling apart.

The outer dress was made from a sleeveless, white nylon nightgown in a large size.

Biblical Woman

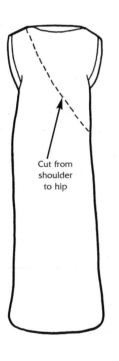

Cut from shoulder to hip

Sleeveless Nightgown

Making the Costume

1. Remove the elastic from the waist of the white linen dress. Press out.

2. Cut the cuffs and neck off a white, long-sleeved turtleneck. Glue at the seams where you cut.

3. Put the white linen dress over the white turtleneck.

4. White nylon nightgown: Cut diagonally across the garment from one shoulder to the opposite hip. Since the nylon won't fray, you need not hem the edge; but again, you should put glue where the seams are sewed together and where you cut.

5. Place white nylon dress over the linen underdress.

6. I used a blue remnant I bought at a discount store for the drape around the head. Make sure you have a piece of fabric that doesn't fray. This will alleviate the need to hem it. Make sure it's large enough to drape around the shoulders.

7. Add sandals or go barefoot.

Greek

Greek Man

Using the same heavy white linen dress used for the underdress of the biblical costumes, I very simply created a Grecian man.

Greek Man

Making the Costume

1. Cut dress to desired length. Glue trim around the hem.

2. Add the same trim from the neck to the hems of sleeves.

3. Garnish a belt with gold fabric paint. Add a headband, arm cuffs and sandals. The lacings for the sandals are made of gold trim glued to the sides.

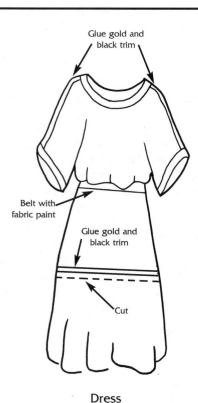

Glue gold and black trim

Belt with fabric paint

Glue gold and black trim

Cut

Dress

Extra-large Linen Dress

Greek Woman

Greek Woman

The Greek woman can be accomplished almost as simply as the man by layering two garments. Since most of the Greeks wore white or pale colors, the same white dress worked well.

Making the Costume

1. White nightgown: Cut diagonally from one shoulder, under the opposite breast and to the hip. Glue edge under. Trim across breast.

2. White linen dress: Cut from the opposite shoulder, under the breast and up to the other shoulder.

3. Split the sleeve on the cut-out side.

4. Cut the hem off to the desired length. Glue trim around the hem.

5. Glue trim down the shoulder of the intact sleeve to the hem. Add bracelets, choker and sandals. Use a chain belt.

Linen Dress

Sleeveless Nightgown

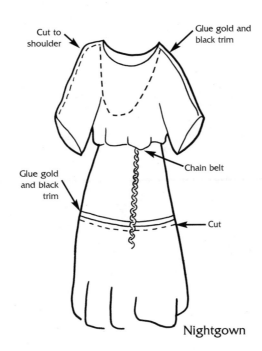

Cut to shoulder

Glue gold and black trim

Glue gold and black trim

Chain belt

Cut

Nightgown

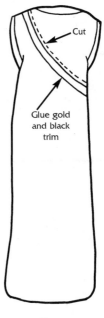

Cut

Glue gold and black trim

Dress

Roman

Roman Man

With Caesar as my inspiration, I found a red robe to use over the versatile white linen dress.

Roman Man

Making the Costume

1. Dress: Loosen the elastic from inside the waist. Press out. Glue trim around the neck and add a brooch in the center.

2. Robe: Cut diagonally from one shoulder to opposite hip in the front. Do the same in the back but leave the fabric attached. Bring it up over the shoulder and glue in place. Cut the hem diagonally.

3. Cut the remaining sleeve off at the elbow and split it to the shoulder.

4. Glue trim to the diagonal hem and the split in the sleeve. Add gold cuffs, sandals and a headdress made of silk leaves.

Linen Dress

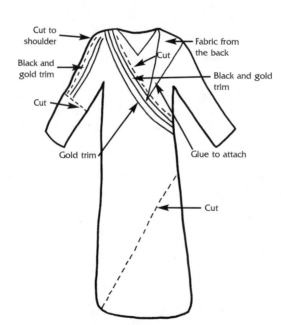

Cut to shoulder

Black and gold trim

Cut

Gold trim

Fabric from the back

Cut

Black and gold trim

Glue to attach

Cut

Dress with Robe

Robe

Roman Woman

Roman Woman

Like the Greek woman's costume, the Roman woman's costume can be created by using two garments for a layered look. I chose a black slip as my undergarment and a black dress to go over it.

Making the Costume

1. Black dress: Tie the sleeves up with pieces of silver trim and glue. Cut the hem diagonally.

2. Glue silver fringe to the hem and silver trim across the bodice. Using the fabric from the cut-off hem, trim with silver fringe and glue to shoulder.

3. Put dress over slip, add a chain belt, necklace and bracelet.

Mid-calf Dress

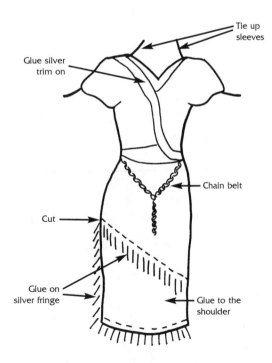

Tie up sleeves

Glue silver trim on

Chain belt

Cut

Glue on silver fringe

Glue to the shoulder

Dress

Full-length Slip

Byzantine

Byzantine Woman

Byzantine Woman

During the Byzantine period, women were still into the layered look. The dress I located already had the layered look; however, it was the wrong color. I achieved the desired color with a bottle of brown dye.

Making the Costume

1. Dye the layered red dress brown. Glue brown fabric diagonally across the chest.

2. Cut the waist off the brown skirt. Sew it to a slip so that it hangs to the ankles. Wear this under the layered dress.

3. Cut the red robe off under the arms. Use the button closure nearest the cut to close at the neck. Glue tucks in the neck.

4. Use scraps from the remaining fabric of the red robe to put around the waist, for cuffs, and to wrap braids. Add chained belts and a horned hat.

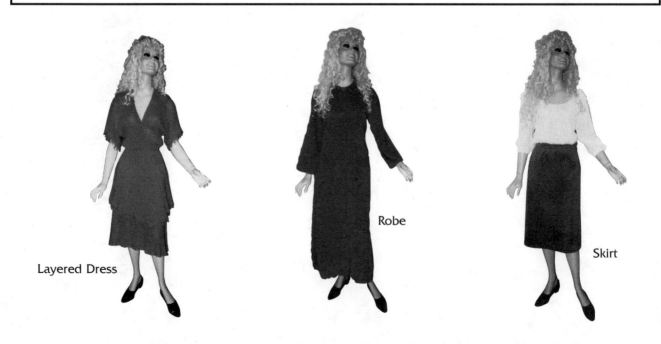

Layered Dress

Robe

Skirt

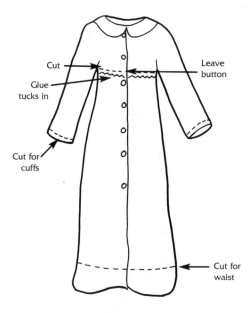

Byzantine Woman
Robe (Cape)

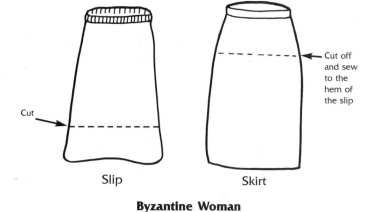

Byzantine Woman

Byzantine Man

Byzantine Man

To accomplish the Byzantine man, I had to find an extra-large dress and a big robe. Since they tended toward fur, I chose a white fur robe that could be dyed the desired color.

Making the Costume

1. Dye the dress with black dye. Dye the robe with brown dye.

2. Cut the dress off to the desired length. Glue silver trim down the front from the neckline to the waist. Glue fur trim to the hem. Add red fabric at the waist from the Byzantine woman's robe. Add belt and sword.

3. Cut the sleeves out of the brown robe beginning the cut farther down.

4. Using scraps of red fabric, tie around the shoulders of the robe.

5. Use the sleeves for your leggings. Turn them upside down so the shoulder is over the feet and the cuff is at the calf. Wrap them with red shoestrings.

6. With both costumes, sandals or old house shoes can be worn.

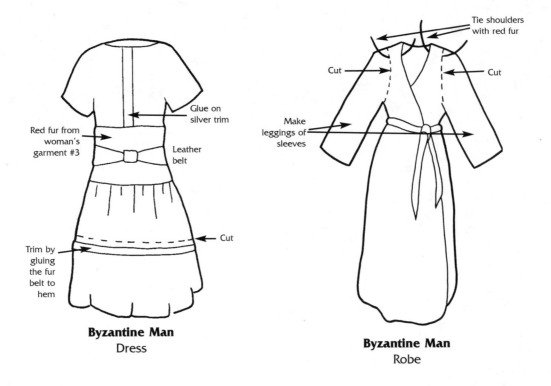

Byzantine Man
Dress

Glue on silver trim

Red fur from woman's garment #3

Leather belt

Cut

Trim by gluing the fur belt to hem

Byzantine Man
Robe

Tie shoulders with red fur

Cut

Cut

Make leggings of sleeves

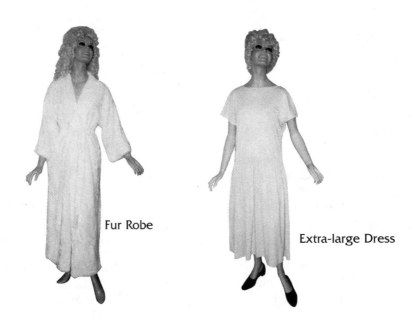

Fur Robe

Extra-large Dress

T I P
The horned hats were purchased. See the resource section at the back of the book. The heavy jewelry can be found at rummage sales, thrift shops and discount stores. Just keep in mind that Byzantines wore heavy-looking gold and silver.

Gothic

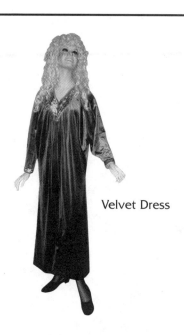

Gothic Woman

Gothic Woman

With a wedding dress, a velvet dress and an old black nylon cape, my Gothic woman was born. It is an intricate and beautiful costume, but it's so simple there will be no need for a diagram.

Making the Costume

1. Dye the wedding dress with a bottle of black dye.

2. Cut the neck out of the wedding dress. The cape is a cheap Halloween cape.

3. Cut the silver trim off the neck of the velvet dress. Glue the cape to it. Hook a long chain at the front point of the silver trim so that the chain can be wrapped and crisscrossed around the body.

4. Using a pillbox-style hat, cover with black trim and use a piece of the velvet dress to drape around the head.

5. Add a silver belt that hangs low on the waist.

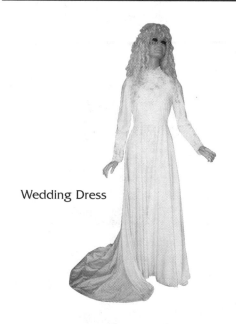

Wedding Dress

Velvet Dress

Gothic Man

I located a great purple dress with the right sleeves, in an extra-large size. With the skirt from an old formal and a lab coat, the Gothic man was simple.

Gothic Man

Making the Costume

1. Purple dress: Cut off the hem. Add lace cuffs to sleeves. Glue trim down the front. Add a wide fabric belt with a decorative belt over it. (I used leather with gold fabric paint trim.)

2. Cut the hem of the lab coat to the desired length. Cut out the front, collar and sleeves, and glue back the edges.

3. Using the collar, tack on a piece of hook-and-loop tape in the back and glue layers of ruffled trim for the neck.

4. The hat was one of those collapsible foam clown hats. I covered it with the leftover fabric from the dress while in a collapsed state and added blue feathers.

5. Add a pair of tights. If you can't find them for men, buy women's queen-size exercise tights. Shoes can be a pair of old house shoes.

6. The cape is made by cutting the skirt out of a formal prom gown. Double it over at the waist and glue it together for that layered look. Glue the edge under, leaving a tie inside. Tie it under the neck ruffle.

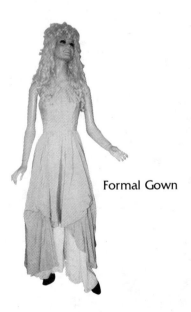

Formal Gown

Lab Coat

Dress

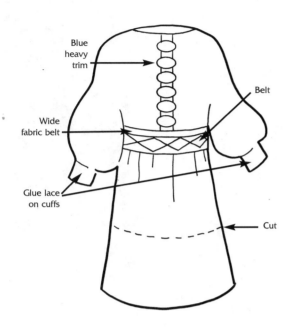

Blue
heavy
trim

Belt

Wide
fabric belt

Glue lace
on cuffs

Cut

Gothic Man
Dress

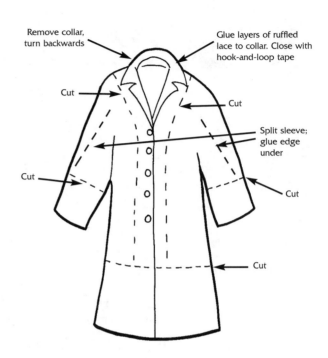

Remove collar,
turn backwards

Glue layers of ruffled
lace to collar. Close with
hook-and-loop tape

Cut

Cut

Split sleeve;
glue edge
under

Cut

Cut

Cut

Cut

Gothic Man
Lab Coat

Renaissance

Renaissance Man

Renaissance Man

Three women's robes that cost me a dollar apiece and a woman's white ruffled blouse that I found at a yard sale were used to create the Renaissance man's costume.

Making the Costume

1. Robe #1: Dye with brown dye. Turn backwards. Glue gold trim and blue plastic jewels to bodice. Add a belt so the robe can be pulled up and have a bloused effect.

2. Robe #2: Cut the front sections out of both sides.

3. Figured robe #3: Remove the collar and lapels all the way to the hem. Cut out the sleeves lower than the armholes. Sew the sections from robe #2 into robe #3, sewing the lapels on in the front.

4. Trim the edges of the robe with gold trim.

5. Using a high-necked ruffled blouse that buttons in the back, add more layers of ruffled lace for the neck.

6. The hat is made by cutting a piece of the figured robe in a circle, stuffing one of the sleeves with fiberfill and twisting it with gold trim. Glue the circle into the center of the sleeve after the ends are glued together.

7. Add blue feathers to the hat and gold buckles made of cardboard and trim to the shoes.

Robe #1

Robe #2

Robe #3 (figured)

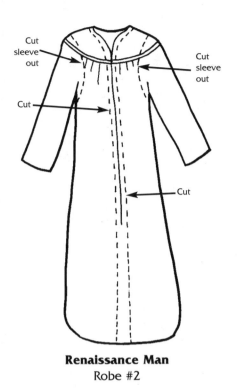

Renaissance Man
Robe #2

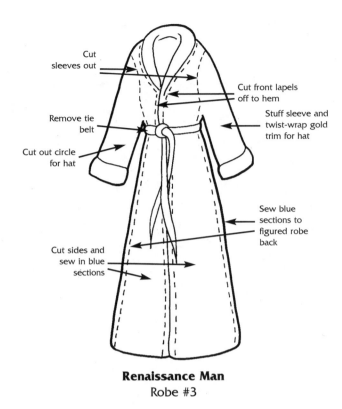

Renaissance Man
Robe #3

Renaissance Woman

Velvet, for some reason, is difficult to find in Arizona. However, I did locate a wonderful red velvet cocktail dress at a rummage sale to be my overdress. Coupled with an old prom dress, it made a beautiful Renaissance woman.

Renaissance Woman

Making the Costume

1. Prom dress: Dye blue. Pull up sleeves from the elbow and glue to just below the shoulder. Glue white ruffle at the neck with a blue plastic jewel at the throat. Glue heavy silver trim down the front center of the dress.

2. Velvet cocktail dress: Split up the front, up the sides to the hips, and up the back to below the zipper. Glue black sequin trim at the edge and around the hole near the neckline. Place it over the prom dress.

3. The hat is made from a stiff net sleeve of a cocktail dress. I simply glued silver trim and a plastic jewel to the sleeve for the desired effect.

4. The arm coverings are a pair of men's nylon white socks with the feet cut out. They work very well, are a non-fray fabric, and will give you a very nice period look.

5. The cape is an old train that went with a wedding dress. I dyed it blue with the prom dress and attached it to the velvet dress, on either side of the zipper, with hook-and-loop tape. Because it was a different fabric, it dyed a bit darker than the dress.

Prom Dress

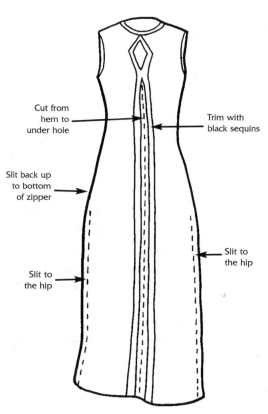

Cut from hem to under hole

Trim with black sequins

Slit back up to bottom of zipper

Slit to the hip

Slit to the hip

Velvet Cocktail Dress

Velvet Cocktail Dress

Elizabethan

Elizabethan Man

Elizabethan Man

Think of kings and courts when you think of the Elizabethan period. The men, although very virile, wore a lot of lace in their court clothes. It is not as difficult as you might imagine to create the look of a ruff around the neck. If you can find a high-necked blouse that fastens in the back, add a piece of white fabric to the neck and glue on layers of ruffled lace, and it will stand up. If you don't have a blouse with the proper neck, cut the collar off a man's white shirt, put the collar up, and glue the ruffled lace on. It will work.

Making the Costume

1. Woman's black suit: Cut the pants off just below the knee and glue a piece of green fabric to the hem. Slit the sleeves almost to the elbow and glue green fabric to the raw edges. Glue ruffles to the bottom of the pants legs.

2. Robe: Cut off at the knee. Cut sleeves out. Glue edges under. Add a belt.

3. Woman's black and white suit: The skirt is a wrap-around. Remove it from the top of the suit and glue the waistband of the skirt to one shoulder of the robe across the back to the waist of the robe.

4. Using a high-necked ruffled blouse that buttons in the back, add more layers of ruffled lace for the neck.

5. Add white nylon stockings, black shoes with green bows and a black felt top hat with a green feather. Most men of the period wore gloves.

Woman's Black Suit

Robe

Black and White Suit

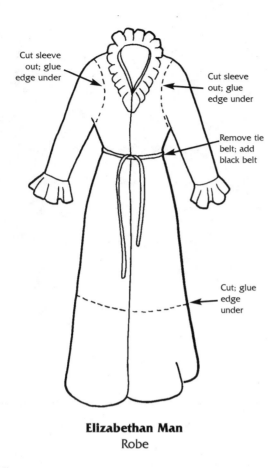

Cut sleeve out; glue edge under

Cut sleeve out; glue edge under

Remove tie belt; add black belt

Cut; glue edge under

Elizabethan Man
Robe

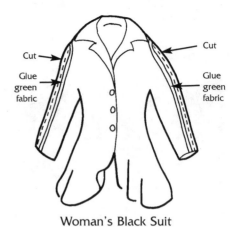

Cut

Cut

Glue green fabric

Glue green fabric

Woman's Black Suit

Glue green fabric

Cut

Glue ruffled lace to hems

Woman's Black Suit

T I P   If you have trouble finding gloves, hats, etc., for men, see the resource section in the back of the book.

Elizabethan Woman

This was one of those costumes that I had to mull over for several days before I figured out an easy way to make it. I explained about the farthingale underskirting on pages 10-12. If you don't understand the picture, reread that section.

Any dress with that much skirting requires some sewing. However, the sewing is a straight line, so there shouldn't be any problem.

Even though I used more garments to build the costume, none of them cost much, so I still spent less than thirty dollars for the costume itself. The hoop skirt I converted into a farthingale came with one of the wedding dresses used for another costume.

Elizabethan Woman

Black Cocktail Dress and
Gold and Black Skirt

Farthingale

Making the Costume

1. Black cocktail dress: Cut off just below the bust, leaving the boning in. Glue the edge under. You may have to bend the boning and pinch with pliers. Remove the colored roses. Cut the skirt leaving it shorter in the front and longer on the sides and in the back.

2. Gold and black skirt, black velvet skirt, black satin skirt: Remove the waist of the gold and black skirt and take out the black tafetta lining. Split the lining in half lengthwise. Sew the lining pieces on each side of the gold and black skirt. Remove the waist of the black satin skirt and slit it lengthwise. Sew a piece on each side of the taffeta skirt. Remove the waist and sew the black velvet skirt to both sides of the satin skirt for the back.

3. Taking tucks as you go, sew the skirts to the hem of the cut-off cocktail dress.

4. Black and white suit: Remove the collar from the jacket and glue it back onto the jacket so the edges go under the arms. You need it to stand up. Glue lace around the top edge of the collar. Put a ruffled, high-necked blouse under the jacket and the jacket under the cocktail dress.

5. I used beading from an old beaded curtain for the necklaces and fixed it at the bodice with a gold brooch.

6. Put the gown over the farthingale underskirt. Since the fabric on the sides is light, it will stand out perfectly.

7. The hat is made from a lady's old wired black hat embellished with gold and black trim and white ruffle.

Black and White Suit

Velvet Skirt

Satin Skirt

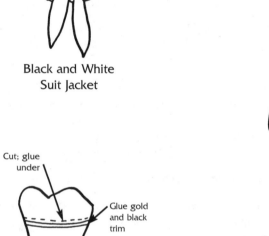

Glue collar on

Remove collar

Remove belt

Black and White
Suit Jacket

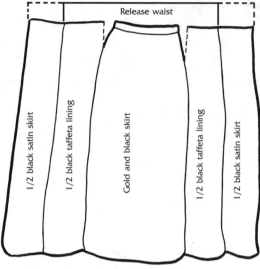

Sew black velvet skirt into the back

Release waist

1/2 black satin skirt

1/2 black taffeta lining

Gold and black skirt

1/2 black taffeta lining

1/2 black satin skirt

Elizabethan Woman
Combination of All Skirts

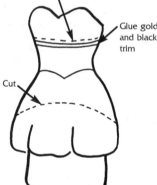

Cut; glue under

Glue gold and black trim

Cut

Cocktail Dress

If you don't have a hoop skirt and can't find one, see the resource section in the back of the book.

T I P

Commonwealth

Commonwealth Man

Commonwealth Man

When I think of the Commonwealth period, I think of cavaliers and pirates. In making the pirate costume for the period, understand that the wealthier men's outfits of the period are a take-off of it. By changing the fabric and how fancy it is, you can make most men's costumes of the period with the same idea.

Making the Costume

1. Red robe: Cut the hem off to the desired length. Glue the lapels back. Glue buttons on both sides of the lapels. Glue the cuffs from the blue smoking jacket onto the sleeves of the red robe.

2. Smoking jacket: Cut the arms out and glue the edges under. Turn the lighter blue lapels and collar under and glue them out of sight. Glue gold buttons on the front of the jacket for appearances only.

3. Place the blue vest and long red jacket over a white ruffled blouse.

4. The ruffled neckpiece can be made by cutting the neck off a man's white shirt just below the top button. Remove the collar. Turn it backwards and glue a piece of fabric to hang down in front. Glue on layers of ruffled lace.

5. Add a wide black belt and tall black boot tops. Boot tops are like a long sock with the feet cut out, but made of leather or leather-like material. I use hook-and-loop tape in the back to hold the boot top.

6. The knee pants can be made from any pair of pants that are cut off, but for that particular period, they look better if they are a bit blousy. Add a sword and tricorn hat with a feather, and you are ready to take to the sea.

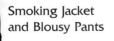

Smoking Jacket
and Blousy Pants

Robe

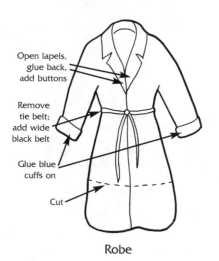

Open lapels, glue back, add buttons

Remove tie belt; add wide black belt

Glue blue cuffs on

Cut

Robe

Turn collar and lapel under and glue

Cut sleeves out; glue edges under

Remove cuffs; glue to red robe

Remove tie belt

Commonwealth Man
Smoking Jacket

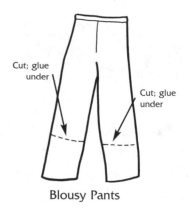

Cut; glue under

Cut; glue under

Blousy Pants

Commonwealth Woman

I attempted to do my Commonwealth woman in the same class as the pirate man for the period. We've all seen her in movies — the young wench that works in the tavern. She wears a mob hat and a corset over a split-skirt dress. It should be seductive without being too revealing.

I located a dress, a slip, and a boned dress that would be perfect for the look I was striving to achieve.

Commonwealth Woman

Making the Costume

1. Dye all three garments with red dye. Because they are made of different fabrics, they will come out in different shades ranging from pink to red.

2. Boned, flowered dress: Cut off where the skirt starts, leaving the boning intact. Cut a vee in the front. Glue the edges under and glue black ruffled lace around the vee and the hem. The zipper is in back and should be fine. If you have a dress that has a longer zipper, remove it and use hook-and-loop tape or hooks and eyes on tape for closure.

Boned Dress

Dress

Slip

3. Pink dress: Split up the front and glue under, making hem smaller at the top and wider at the skirt.

4. Slip: Glue a brooch on the slip at the vee of the bodice.

5. Putting it together: The slip goes on first, then the dress. Add the boned dress top last.

6. You will want something to make the dress stand out on the sides. I used throw pillows glued and pinned to an underskirt.

7. Add a choker necklace and make a mob hat from the skirt of the flowered dress. Add black slippers.

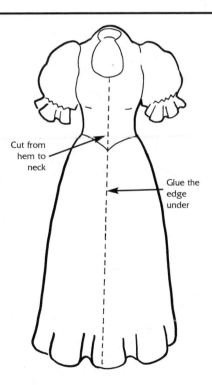

Cut from hem to neck

Glue the edge under

Dress

42

Restoration

Restoration Man

Restoration Man

The men's costumes of the Restoration period are very similar to the costumes of the Commonwealth period, with perhaps more lace and feathers. For the Restoration man, I purchased a woman's fall coat and a wrap-around dress.

Keep in mind that when using women's dresses for men's costumes you must cut the armholes larger than they are to allow for the larger upper arm and wider back.

Woman's Fall Coat

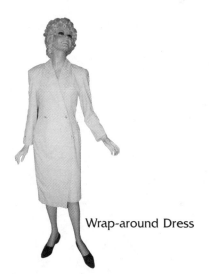

Wrap-around Dress

Making the Costume

1. Coat: Remove the buttons. Cut hem to desired length. Split the sleeves to just below the shoulders. Trim hem and split sleeves with dark blue trim. Glue back lapels and glue on gold buttons. Hold lapels back by gluing on a small piece of gray fabric midway down the coat.

2. Dress: Cut the sleeves out, cutting larger armholes. Bring lapels together and fasten with hook-and-loop tape. Cut the hem so it falls at the top of the legs. Glue trim around armholes and hem. Except for the one button in use, glue buttons on the front in two rows.

3. Use a pair of women's white stretch pants cut off below the knee for the short tight pants. Use the lace from the collar of the wrap-around dress to glue on the hem of the pants.

4. Add a white ruffled blouse.

5. The ruffle that hangs from the neck is accomplished by gluing a piece of fabric to a man's reversed collar and gluing rows of lace to it. Make sure that when you cut the collar off, you leave the top button for closure.

6. Add a tricorn hat with feathers, and glue some buckles on a pair of black shoes. The stockings are men's nylon hose purchased at a discount store.

Restoration Man

Close collar

Split sleeves

Glue small piece of gray fabric to hold back lapel

Cut; glue edge under

Trim with dark blue trim

Remove buttons; fold back lapels; glue on gold buttons

Trim with dark blue trim

Cut; glue edge under

Cut

Coat

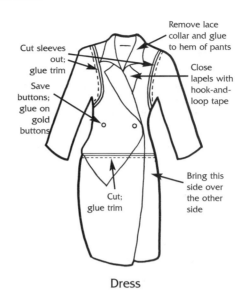

Cut sleeves out; glue trim

Save buttons; glue on gold buttons

Remove lace collar and glue to hem of pants

Close lapels with hook-and-loop tape

Bring this side over the other side

Cut; glue trim

Dress

Restoration Woman

Restoration Woman

I located three dresses, which when put together make a beautiful Restoration gown. I threw all three dresses in the washer with a mixture of brown and red dye to get the unusual color. Because the gowns were made of different fabrics and had lace on them, I achieved several shades of the same color.

Making the Costume

1. Dye all three dresses together with brown and red dye.

2. Dress with red bows: This is the main gown. Split the skirt to just below the waist and glue the sides back. Pin the top skirt up to the waist on both sides so the lace flows down the skirt. Glue buttons down the front, add a brooch at the neckline, and glue the applique from the neckline of the lace-covered gown to the waist. Make sure you glue far enough around to cover the pins that hold the outer skirt up.

3. Lace-covered gown: Cut the skirt off above the waist leaving the zipper down. Glue the edge under.

4. Lace dress: This dress will be the second layer dress. You would put the lace-covered gown skirt on, then the second layer dress and finally the main dress. If you attach pillows to the side of the second layer dress before you put the main gown over it, you will get the desired effect of the period.

5. Add a choker, long gloves and feathers for the hair.

6. For the white powder wigs, see the resource section at the back of the book.

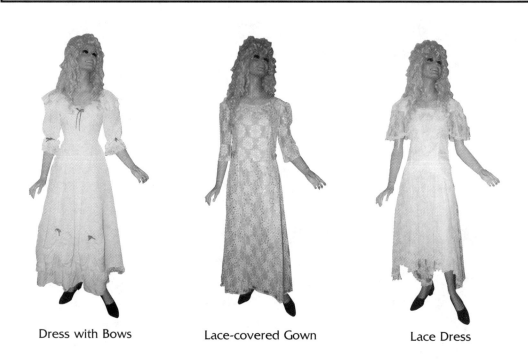

Dress with Bows   Lace-covered Gown   Lace Dress

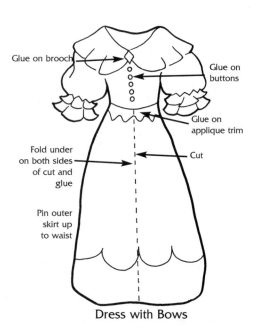

Glue on brooch

Glue on buttons

Glue on applique trim

Fold under on both sides of cut and glue

Cut

Pin outer skirt up to waist

Dress with Bows

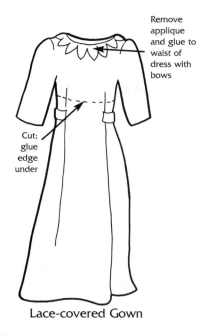

Remove applique and glue to waist of dress with bows

Cut; glue edge under

Lace-covered Gown

Georgian

Georgian Man

Georgian Man

The redcoats are coming! Paul Revere rode from farmhouse to farmhouse and village to village crying out this warning, and this is what the British soldiers may have been wearing.

Making the Costume

1. Woman's red trench coat: Cut the collar off, leaving a short stand-up collar. Fold the lapels back. Using blue non-fray fabric, glue the fabric on so it shows on both sides. Glue on blue cuffs to match.

2. Using scrap fabric from the gold robe used on the Egyptian man, I cut strips and glued them on the front of the jacket. The buttons are made of gold fabric paint. Do the same at the collar and cuffs. Glue white ruffled lace inside the cuffs.

3. Woman's vest: Remove the button and sew on a gold button in its place. Glue matching buttons down the front of the vest.

Woman's Trench Coat

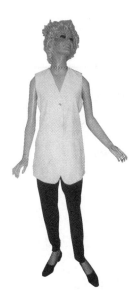

Woman's Vest

Glue on blue and gold fabric

Cut off collar and leave a small stand-up collar

Remove belt

Fold lapels back and glue on blue and gold fabric

Glue blue fabric to both cuffs; lace inside

Remove original buttons; add gold fabric paint buttons

Fold back farther as you go down; continue fold even into the red coat

Georgian Man
Woman's Trench Coat

4. Use a pair of women's white stretch pants cut off at the knee. Glue a strip of the blue fabric to the hem.

5. Man's ruffled neckpiece: Use the same method as for the Commonwealth and Restoration men (pages 39 and 42).

6. Add white nylon hose, a tricorn hat with feathers and buckles on the shoes.

7. In your search for a white powder wig, see the resource section of this book.

T I P

The shoe buckles are made from strips of cardboard glued together to form a rectangle and covered with gold trim. You can use sticky-backed hook-and-loop tape to fasten them to the shoes, or you can glue them directly to the shoes.

Georgian Tavern Wench

Georgian Tavern Wench

I used three garments from the Commonwealth woman's costume for this dress. I also used a beige nightshirt. The tavern wench is the same idea as the Commonwealth woman with a few changes.

When the British soldier was hot and sweaty after a day of fighting, he may have been tempted to buy a pint in the local tavern. This is what the serving girl may have worn.

Making the Costume

1. Dye the long slip, the pink dress and the floral dress in red dye for three cycles. They are different fabrics, so they will dye in various shades.

2. Slip and pink dress: Leaving the zippers down, cut off above the waist and glue the edges under. Two small throw pillows attached to the underskirt will give you the full look on the sides. The fabric of the dress is lightweight but heavy enough to fall nicely.

Slip   Dress   Floral Dress   Nightshirt

3. Floral dress: Cut in a deep vee at the bodice and cut the skirt off at the hip. Glue black lace trim to the bodice and hem. If the zipper was not left in place, use hook-and-loop tape or hooks and eyes on tape for closure in the back.

4. Nightshirt: Leave the front long to act as your apron. Cut off the neck ruffle. Slit up the sides to the waist, glue the edges under and tuck in the back.

5. Putting it together: Put on the slip, followed by the dress. Add the nightshirt and then the floral dress top. Add a choker and a mob hat.

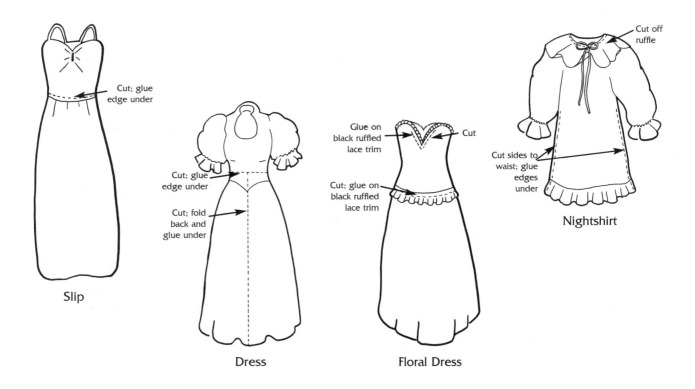

Slip

Dress

Floral Dress

Nightshirt

Georgian Woman

The gown I chose for the Georgian woman could be worn to court or to a ball. It is very elaborate but was relatively simple to make. I took four white dresses I had on hand and put them together to make the Georgian gown.

Georgian Woman

Making the Costume

1. Sequined gown: Cut off above the waist. Cut out side seams so that you have two sections of skirt.

2. Short dress: Cut off just below the bust. Glue the edge under. Cut off the hem, leaving very little in front but most of the skirt on the sides and back. Cut a triangle of sequined material out of the sequined dress and glue to the front. Trim hem at top and trim at hip.

3. Sequin and chiffon dress: Cut the chiffon overskirt out and separate into two skirts. Do the same with the white satin lining.

4. Sew the skirt sections together as shown in the diagram.

5. Wedding dress: Remove the train. Cut the center section of lace out of the bodice and glue white trim there. I glued a white sequined applique between the breasts. Cut the hem off just below the back zipper and glue the edge under. Cut off the sleeves above the elbow and glue a wide piece of ruffled lace at the hem.

6. Sew the skirting to the hem of the short white dress, taking tucks where needed.

7. Putting it together: The wedding dress goes on first. The underskirting goes on second. What was made from the short white dress with all the skirting goes on last. Add a choker and a white powder wig to complete the look.

Sequined Gown

Short Dress

Underskirting

Sequin and Chiffon Dress

Wedding Dress

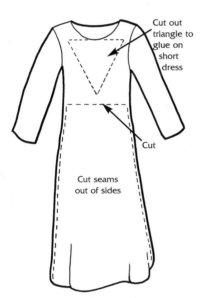

Cut out triangle to glue on short dress

Cut

Cut seams out of sides

Sequined Gown

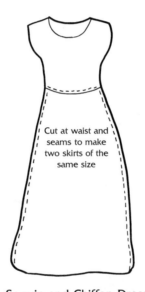

Cut at waist and seams to make two skirts of the same size

Sequin and Chiffon Dress

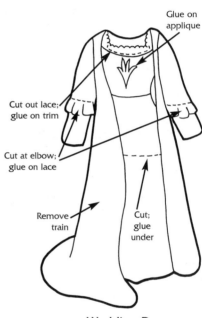

Glue on applique

Cut out lace; glue on trim

Cut at elbow; glue on lace

Remove train

Cut; glue under

Wedding Dress

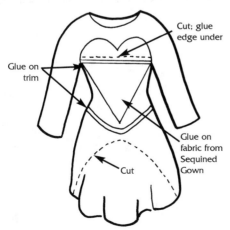

Cut; glue edge under

Glue on trim

Glue on fabric from Sequined Gown

Cut

Short Dress

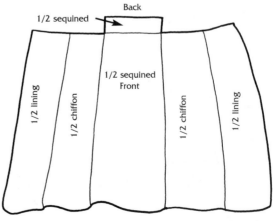

Back

1/2 sequined

1/2 lining

1/2 chiffon

1/2 sequined Front

1/2 chiffon

1/2 lining

Skirt Arrangement

Romantic

Romantic Man

I've found that many men's costumes can be made easily and cheaply by using an old suit. I found an old, black, double-breasted suit for the Romantic man. The vest was quite a find. I was in Buffalo, Missouri, visiting my father when I located it in a second-hand store. It was perfect for my men's costumes, and I was able to use it for several, as you will see.

Romantic Man

Making the Costume

1. Suit: Remove the original buttons. Cut the jacket off just below the waist and glue the edge under. Remember that if the garment is lined, you must glue the lining to the fabric before you glue the edge under. Tack a piece of hook-and-loop tape to the lapel to hold it together. Remove original buttons and glue a set of eight buttons on the front.

2. Suit pants: Since you will be cutting the legs out of the pants, they do not have to fit. Cut one leg out of the pants just below the crotch. Press the crease out. Cut it in half lengthwise, and glue the edges under. Glue the tails into the back of the jacket, underneath the hem, beginning at the sides.

3. The vest should be long enough to hang in front of the jacket hem.

4. Add a contrasting pair of pants. I used a dark gray. Add a neck ruffle (see pages 39 and 42). A white shirt, gloves, spats made of socks and a top hat complete the costume. I added a walking stick.

Suit

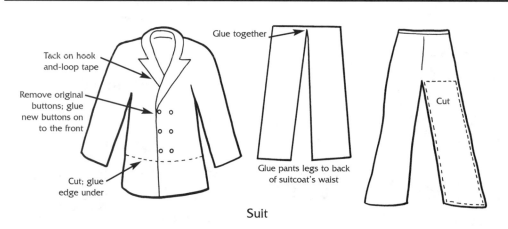

Tack on hook and-loop tape

Remove original buttons; glue new buttons on to the front

Cut; glue edge under

Glue together

Glue pants legs to back of suitcoat's waist

Cut

Suit

Vest

Romantic Woman

Shorter Dress

Longer Dress

Romantic Woman

A mixture of pink and black dye was used for the two white dresses for this costume. The shorter dress had the large sleeves I wanted for the period gown but the longer dress had the length I needed, so I combined the two.

Making the Costume

1. Dye the two dresses together with a bottle of pink and a bottle of black dye.

2. Shorter dress: Glue the zig-zag design under the neckline. Pull the skirt up, rolling the hem under at the sides until you get to just behind the waist. Pin it and put glue over the pin. Cover it in the folds of the fabric.

3. Normally I would cut the sleeves off the longer dress, but for this particular gown we won't be doing that. The puffy sleeves will help to hold out the bigger sleeves from the shorter gown.

4. Trim the ruffle off around the neckline. Remove the sash tie. Bring one side of the first layer skirting across the front of the dress to the opposite hip and pin. Cover the pin with glue and fabric.

5. Tie a white sash tie at the waist. Use the dyed tie to make a ribbon for the hair.

6. Add long white gloves and a choker necklace. The necklace is made from a piece of trim fastened in back with hook-and-loop tape and a brooch pinned in the center.

Remove neck ruffle

Remove tie belt for the hair

Longer Dress

Bring hem to opposite hip and pin. Glue and pinch into folds of fabric

Glue the zig zag under

Remove tie belt before dyeing

Bring hem to the waist, rolling under at the sides; pin. Cover the pins at the waist with glue and pinch into the folds of the fabric

Shorter Dress

Old West

Old West Man

I used the same suit as for the Romantic man to make a frock coat for a man from the Old West. The same vest worked well for this costume, too.

Old West Man

Making the Costume

1. Black suit: Cut the pants off at the crotch. Press the creases out of the legs. Turn them upside down so that the hem of the pants is at the top. Glue the edge of the two pieces together a few inches down. Glue around the waist of the jacket just under the second button.

2. The same pants, shirt and vest will work with the costume. Add a string tie and a western-style hat.

Suit

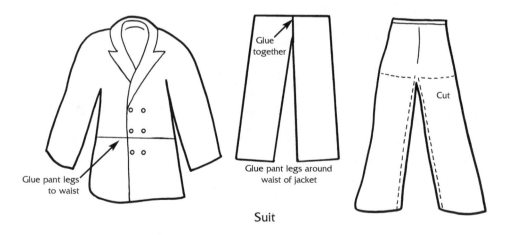

Glue pant legs to waist

Glue together

Glue pant legs around waist of jacket

Cut

Suit

Vest

Old West Man #2 (Piano Player)

The Old West piano player can be accomplished by using a pair of pants, a white shirt and a vest. Add a pair of arm garters, a black string tie and a derby hat. I added a toy gun found at a rummage sale.

This costume can be used for a storekeeper or town person for a play or as a character in a parade.

> See the resource section at the back of the book for hats, garters and string ties.
>
> **T I P**

**Old West Man #2
Piano Player**

Dance Hall Girl

As you can see by now, I like to use old wedding gowns whenever I can find them reasonably priced. They have a great deal of skirting and can be dyed most any color; therefore, they are adaptable to many costumes.

The wedding dress used for the Dance Hall girl was located at a second-hand store in Wickenburg, Arizona, and purchased for twenty-two dollars. I chose it for this particular costume because of the neckline and the layers of lace ruffle in the skirt.

I came up with the orange/red color by mixing red and yellow dye and running it through three cycles of the washer. The longer you run your garment through cycles, the more brilliant the color will be.

Dance Hall Girl

Making the Costume

1. Dye gown with a bottle of red and a bottle of yellow dye through three cycles.

2. Cut out the lace sleeves and the lace at the neck.

3. Glue sequin trim and long gold fringe to the bodice and short front skirt. Add a fancy belt.

4. Cut straight up the center of the skirt to the top layer of ruffled lace. Underneath the first layer of lace, cut the skirting to the seams on both sides. Glue underneath the back of the dress.

5. Bring the edges of the top layer of lace up to the waist and pin and glue. Cover the pins with trim.

6. The feathers for the headpiece are glued to a wide, black-fabric headband.

7. Add long gloves, a choker made of black sequin trim with a brooch in the center, and a red feather boa.

Cut out neck and both armholes

Gold fringe on both shoulders

Black sequin trim

Belt

Gold fringe

Cut; glue underneath the back of the skirt

Dance Hall Girl
Wedding Gown

Dance Hall Girl
Wedding Gown

Cowboy

Cowboy costumes are pretty common and easy to make, so I thought I would show you how to make a pair of chaps from a couple of skirts. For some reason, the picture of skirt #1 looks like a different color in the picture than it looks in the final picture. I have no idea what caused that, but I assure you it is the skirt I used.

Cowboy

Making the Costume

1. Skirt #1: Leaving the waist intact, cut the back of the skirt out.

2. Cut lengthwise so you have two separate sections.

3. Cut up to the crotch in the front of the skirt. Glue the back sections on the bottom of the front. Trim so they are rounded at the bottom.

4. Cut skirt #2 in wide strips, glue to the chaps and fringe.

5. Add a plaid shirt, a vest, scarf, hat, gun and boots.

6. Use the scraps from skirt #2 to make a loop of fabric at the back of the legs to hold the chaps in place.

Skirt #1   Skirt #2   Shirt

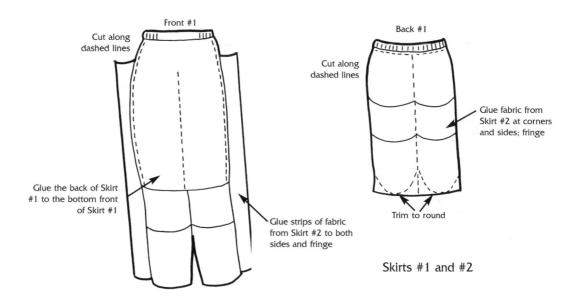

Front #1
Cut along dashed lines

Back #1
Cut along dashed lines

Glue fabric from Skirt #2 at corners and sides; fringe

Glue the back of Skirt #1 to the bottom front of Skirt #1

Glue strips of fabric from Skirt #2 to both sides and fringe

Trim to round

Skirts #1 and #2

Prairie Woman

Prairie Woman

When the cowboy went to a barn dance, he may have found a woman dressed in this costume.

Making the Costume

1. Dress: Cut the lace out of the neck and off the bodice. Add underskirting, and put the white skirt over the dress for an apron look.

2. The bonnet is made by cutting part of the brim off a straw hat and covering it.

Prairie Woman
Dress

Prairie Woman
Skirt

Old West Lady

Old West Lady

This is an absolutely gorgeous gown that was made so simply that I'm almost embarrased to tell you how.

The wedding dress was purchased at a second-hand store for fifteen dollars, and the yellow dye cost under six dollars. I ran it through two cycles of yellow dye to achieve the right color. Because the lace was made of a different fabric, it dyed darker to give it that wonderful contrast.

Making the Costume

1. Dye the wedding dress yellow.

2. Pick the dress up at the start of the ruffled lace on one side and bring it across the dress to the opposite hip. Pin and glue it.

3. Glue black sequin trim around the waist. Make sure you go over the pin to hide it. Glue the same trim up the front and around the neckline and at the cuffs.

4. The hat was a woman's felt hat. I cut the brim off and decorated it with black sequin trim, feathers and flowers.

5. Add a choker, a looser necklace and a pair of black shoes.

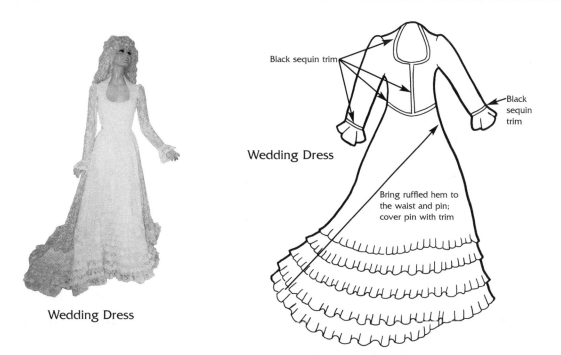

Wedding Dress

Black sequin trim

Black sequin trim

Wedding Dress

Bring ruffled hem to the waist and pin; cover pin with trim

TIP

If you have trouble finding feathers, see the resource section at the back of the book.

Crinoline
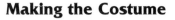

Crinoline Woman

Shades of Scarlett! We are back in the days of the Civil War when men were soldiers and women wore ruffles, lace and frilly bonnets. I found a wedding dress layered with rows of lace that was perfect for my Crinoline woman.

Crinoline Woman

Making the Costume

1. Dye the wedding gown with two bottles of orange dye. Let it go through three cycles for a more brilliant color.

2. Cut the sleeves off just below the shoulder, leaving a small cap sleeve. Turn under hem and glue.

3. Cut the lace off the neck.

4. Glue white ruffled lace around the neckline. Add a pearl brooch at the center.

5. Cut the bottom layer off the back of the dress. Save the orange lace to use on the bonnet. Glue the hem under.

6. Cut the ruffles off the sleeves and glue to a pair of short white gloves.

7. Using a full-brimmed straw hat, cut the back of the brim off. Cover the hat with the orange lace and white ruffled lace. Add silk flowers where you attach the orange tie. Add a pearl choker necklace.

8. Add a hoop skirt. If you don't have one and choose not to purchase one, see page 11 on how to make one easily and cheaply.

Cut lace out of neckline

Add brooch

Cut sleeves out

Glue on ruffle

Cut off cuff ruffles and glue to gloves

Cut off train; glue hem under

Wedding Dress

Wedding Dress

Crinoline Man
Frock Coat

Union Soldier

Confederate Soldier

Crinoline Man (Frock Coat)

Men wore many styles of coats during the Crinoline period, but I had to choose one so I chose the frock coat. It is essentially the same jacket I made for the Old West man (see page 52). By changing the pants to black and adding different accessories, it is the perfect complement to the orange Crinoline woman's costume.

Union Soldier

A frock coat was used for the Union Army during the Civil War. The difference is that the lapel is closed completely, the collar cut off so it makes a small stand-up collar, and the collar and cuffs are decorated with gold trim. Because the jacket is held closed by hook-and-loop tape, you can glue the buttons on the front of the jacket.

The sash was made from leftover fabric from the gold robe I used on the Egyptian man. Add a gold buckled belt, white gloves and a hat.

When I bought the suit, I bought an extra pair of navy blue pants. I glued gold trim up the legs to the bottom of the pockets. You might add a sword.

Union Soldier
Suit

Confederate Soldier

For the Confederate soldier, I purchased a gray suit and a pair of navy blue pants. The frock coat was made the same as the last two. I covered the collar and cuffs with scraps of gold fabric left over from the Egyptian man costume. I also cut strips out of the fabric to glue on the outside legs of the navy pants.

The buttons are done differently on this jacket. I sewed on the bottom two center buttons, tacked hook-and-loop tape at the neck, and glued on the remaining buttons.

I found the design on the cuffs in a picture and copied it in pencil on the arms. I glued braided gold trim to the design.

Add a gold sash, belt, gray gloves and hat. You might want to add a sword.

Confederate Soldier
Suit

Bustle

Bustle Woman

Bustle Woman

If you can find a wedding dress with a train, you're half-way to making a bustle dress. I purchased a wedding dress with a high neck, long sleeves and a reasonably long train. Because the lace on the gown was made of a different fabric, when I dyed the gown with a bottle of black dye, I ended up with a gray dress with black trim. I really liked the way the dress turned out.

The second dress I used is made of a crinkled-up stretchy fabric. Since it was non-fray, I didn't have to worry about gluing under the edges as long as I cut cleanly.

Making the Costume

1. Wedding dress: Dye with one bottle of black dye through two cycles.

2. Black stretchy dress: With the zipper down, cut off at the waist. Leaving the waist intact, cut a "U" out of the front of the skirt and cut a straight line down the front from the bottom of the "U" to the hem. Cut across to the seam on each side.

3. Pull the fabric to the back of the skirt and glue underneath. It will nicely hang down the back of the skirt for that extra bustle look.

4. Glue a large ruffle to the "U" and to the front hem of the wedding dress.

5. Glue wide silver trim at the waist and attach to two strands of fabric to make a bow in the back.

6. By using two underskirts, you can accomplish the bustle look easily. To the back of one underskirt, pin and glue on the second underskirt that has been doubled over twice at the waistband. It will hang down the back to give you that nice long sweep. Add a small hat with feathers and jewelry.

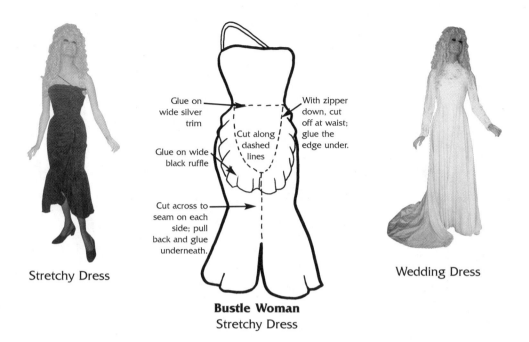

Glue on wide silver trim

With zipper down, cut off at waist; glue the edge under.

Cut along dashed lines

Glue on wide black ruffle

Cut across to seam on each side; pull back and glue underneath.

Bustle Woman
Stretchy Dress

Stretchy Dress

Wedding Dress

Bustle Man

Bustle Man (Cutaway)

As with most men's costumes of the period, I started with a suit. It is pretty easy to find inexpensive suits in the second-hand stores and at rummage sales. I paid five dollars for this particular suit. The only thing you need to watch for is that the pants match the jacket.

To complement my bustle woman's dress, I chose to do a man's cutaway jacket with contrasting pants.

Making the Costume

1. Suit pants: Cut the legs off at the crotch. Cut them down the inseams. Press the creases out and glue the edges under. At one corner, glue the two legs together.

2. Glue the pants to the jacket just below the first button. Glue down the front of the jacket. Pull fabric under until it has that cutaway look, and glue under in front and back.

3. Add a pair of contrasting pants, a long vest, white shirt, hat and gloves.

4. The ascot tie is made by draping a piece of fabric over a piece of thin elastic. Glue in place and tie in back. I glued a rhinestone on the front to look like a stick pin.

Bustle Man
Suit

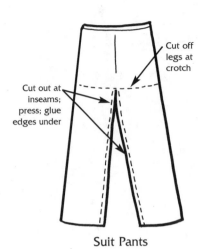

Cut off
legs at
crotch

Cut out at
inseams;
press; glue
edges under

Suit Pants

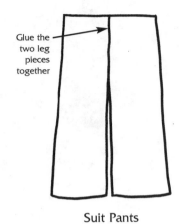

Glue the
two leg
pieces
together

Suit Pants

Glue legs
to waist
in back

Fold back
sides and
glue under
in front

Suit Coat

End of the Century

End of the Century Woman

End of the Century Woman

Bustles were out and big sleeves were in by the turn of the century. Since I couldn't find a long gown with the big sleeves I needed for the dress, I chose a short dress and used the layered look to achieve my goal.

Making the Costume

1. Dye the two dresses at the same time with a bottle of brown dye and a third of a bottle of black dye. I loved the color I got.
2. Short dress: Bring the skirt up and glue wide black trim down the front to hold it in place. Do the same in the back from the bottom of the zipper. Glue rhinestones on intermittently for buttons. Glue the same black trim at the neck and cuffs. Glue a lace appliqué and brooch at the neck.
3. Wedding dress: With the zipper down, cut off the two-layered skirt. Glue the edge under. Split outer skirt a few inches below the waist. With a large safety pin, bring the thin outer skirt to the waist, rolling it under. Pin to the top of the skirt and cover with glue and a piece of fabric. It won't show.
4. I found a black felt hat with a brim on sale at one of those mall jewelry shops. By adding a tie and feather, I could cock it to one side and give it the old-fashioned look I desired.
5. Add an underskirt.

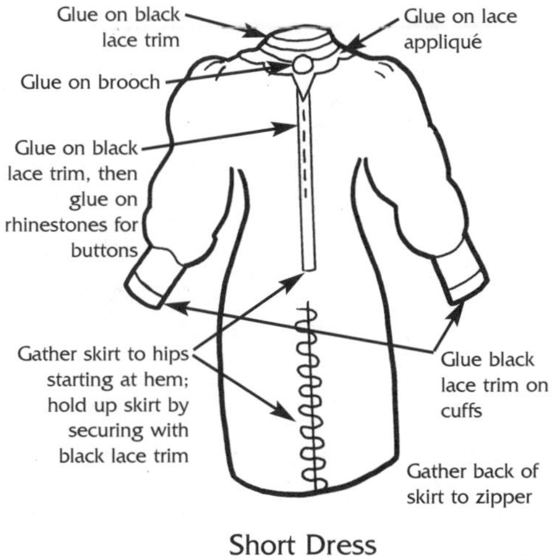
Glue on black lace trim
Glue on lace appliqué
Glue on brooch
Glue on black lace trim, then glue on rhinestones for buttons
Gather skirt to hips starting at hem; hold up skirt by securing with black lace trim
Glue black lace trim on cuffs
Gather back of skirt to zipper

Short Dress

Wedding Dress
Secure rolled sides with pins; glue fabric over
Split outer skirt a few inches below the waist; roll outer skirt under on both sides
With zipper down, cut off above waist; glue the edge under.

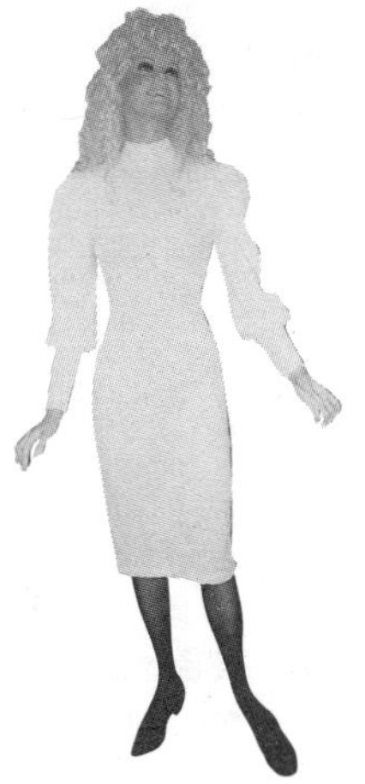

Short Dress

Wedding Dress

End of the Century Man

Gone were the tails, frock coats and cutaway coats at the century's end, except for formal wear. Men were moving into a more comfortable, less formal look. Now that they were driving motor cars, they needed more functional clothing.

I found a small-checked, black and white suit. All that really had to be done to convert the suit was to close the lapel higher, tack on hook-and-loop tape, and glue on two extra buttons.

End of the Century Man

You can profoundly change the look of a suit by the hat and tie you put with it. I chose a derby and bow tie for my costume.

From the end of the century, men's costumes would forever change, never to go back again. The only time tails and cutaways were acceptable was at formal gatherings or weddings. I guess they thought if women were getting away from the uncomfortable underskirting and bustles with the cinched-in waists, they could do it too.

Remember that this costume is but one that a man might wear during the period. Another type would be the Norfolk. It is a jacket again, buttoned up high, but with knickers and white socks. Add a newsboy hat, and you have it. The knickers are a pair of sweat pants pulled up.

I think of this period as a time of experimentation. Men were trying all sorts of new looks.

End of the Century Man
The Norfolk

Suit

Original Suit
for The Norfolk

New Century

New Century Woman

New Century Woman

I had a really ugly dress donated to me by a friend. I hung it in a place where I had to walk past it every day and assured myself I would eventually have some divine inspiration, even though I wasn't convinced.

I was on a trip home to Mattoon, Illinois, when inspiration struck. I saw this jacket in a thrift shop, and it immediately told me that it would work with the dress with very few changes.

Making the Costume

1. Using a bottle of brown and a dash of red, dye the dress. It will give it a richer color, more like a copper.

2. The dress: Cut off the sleeves and the flounce. Glue the edges of the sleeves under.

3. Glue the flounce to the jacket and glue the edge under to make it even.

4. Add a brooch and necklace to the jacket. The hat is a woman's felt hat with a couple of black feathers. I used high-heeled boot shoes and added a walking stick.

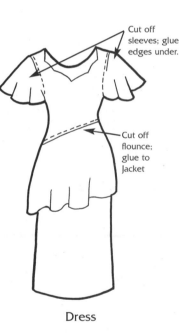

Cut off sleeves; glue edges under.

Cut off flounce; glue to Jacket

Dress

Dress

Jacket

New Century Man
Sack Suit

New Century Man (Sack Suit)

Three-piece Suit

I located a three-piece plaid suit at a second-hand store. With minor changes, it suited my purpose well. I pulled the lapels together closer to the neck and held them with hook-and-loop tape. The top two buttons were glued on. I added a bow tie, a white shirt, and a straw boater and had a nice imitation.

Gibson Girl

The ideal American woman who went to work out in the world — that was the Gibson Girl. Her outfit was high-necked, with an ankle-length skirt. It was more comfortable than the cinched-in waists and big sleeves of the end-of-the-century women. Hats became simpler, too.

Gibson Girl

Making the Costume

1. The white dress: I removed the bow in back to use for the back of the hair.

2. The black skirt: The skirt was perfect, except for the length. I located a similar skirt, cut the bottom out of it, and sewed it to the first one. The buttons up the front of the skirt gave it a nice Gibson Girl look. The second skirt had no buttons, but that wasn't noticeable at the bottom.

3. The suspenders were taken from a pair of pants found at a thrift shop. I transferred the suspender buttons from the pants to the skirt, and it took on the look I wanted.

4. I added a black tie and put a black ribbon and bow around a straw boater. The shoes were high-heeled boot shoes.

Dress   Skirt   Suspender
Pants

Skirt #1

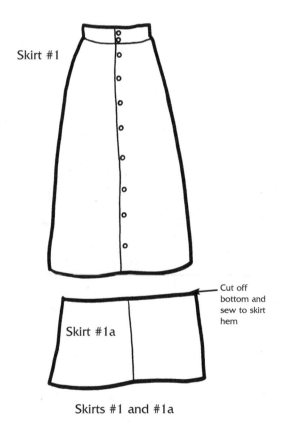

Cut off
bottom and
sew to skirt
hem

Skirt #1a

Skirts #1 and #1a

World War I

**World War I
Woman and Man**

World War I Man and Woman

Because I used a soldier suit for the man, there is no need to show any work. You can still find World War I military wear in pretty good condition in many of the second-hand salvage stores for reasonable prices. Altogether I paid twenty-two dollars for mine. The helmet needed a bit of a paint job, but the suit and the leggings were in good shape.

For the woman, I found a dress and a skirt I could combine to make the right kind of dress.

Making the Costume

1. White dress: Remove the belt and clip off the belt loops. That will give you extra inches in length and the dropped waistline that was in style.

2. Skirt: Because we still need length in the skirt, cut the waist off and sew the remainder of the skirt to a slip.

3. Put the white dress over the blue and white plaid skirt and add a long chain necklace. Add white short gloves and a felt hat.

Dress

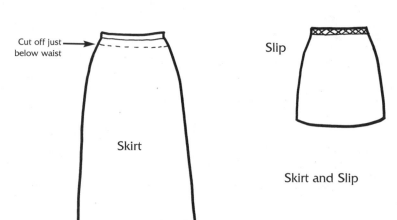

Cut off just
below waist →

Skirt

Slip

Skirt and Slip

Skirt

1920s

1920s Woman

1920s Woman

The 1920s is one of my favorite periods for which to make costumes. When I think of the Twenties, I think of flappers, bathtub gin, gangsters and sultry singers in speakeasies. It was a flashy time when women's outfits were covered with sequins and fringe and men wore fedoras and spats.

I did four costumes from the period to give you an idea of what might have been worn during that time period.

The first was made from two dresses. I found the little black dress in a second-hand store in Prescott, Arizona, and the second in a boutique that was selling out its cocktail dresses.

Making the Costume

1. Black dress: Glue black sequins around the neckline and under the breasts. Glue black fringe on top of the armholes.

2. Cut off the bottom section of the gold and black dress. Glue it to the hips of the little black dress. Glue sequin trim where the skirt is glued to the dress.

3. Add long black gloves, beads and a cigarette holder. The hat is a woman's black velvet hat I found at a rummage sale. I added a black bow and gold brooch. Pull it low around the face.

Cocktail Dress

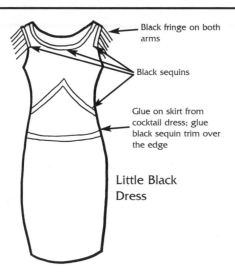

Black fringe on both arms

Black sequins

Glue on skirt from cocktail dress; glue black sequin trim over the edge

Little Black Dress

Cut off skirt; glue to little black dress

Cocktail Dress

Little Black Dress

1920s Gangster

When I think of gangsters, I think of pinstriped suits. I went in search of one and located it in a thrift shop in Wickenburg, Arizona. I picked up a red shirt and black tie to go with it.

Since I couldn't find a double-breasted suit, I will show you how to turn a single-breasted suit into a double-breasted suit with very little effort. You should keep in mind that the suit you buy must be large enough through the body to overlap.

1920s Gangster

Pinstriped Suit

Making the Costume

1. Remove the existing buttons.

2. Make sure you have a least four matching buttons.

3. Sew two buttons farther over on the jacket, overlapping the lapels. Glue the other two buttons next to them. You can do it with six or eight buttons if you wish.

4. Add a red shirt, black tie, fedora hat and spats made with socks.

Flapper

Flapper

Flappers are fun and easy to do. You can make them from any number of different style dresses or even slips. I chose the pink and black dress to show you that you can make a flapper from an unlikely looking dress.

Making the Costume

1. Cut the flounce off the waist and the big bow off the side of the bodice. Cut the skirt to the desired length. Keep in mind that the bottom row of fringe will add a few inches.

2. Alternating pink and orange, glue on long fringe starting at the hem. After each row of fringe, glue on orange sequins. Work your way up to just below the chest but above the waist. It will give you the look of no waist. Glue sequins at the neckline.

Dress

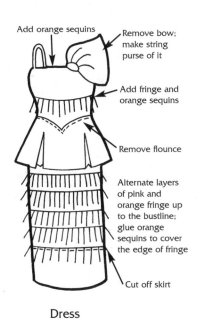

Add orange sequins

Remove bow; make string purse of it

Add fringe and orange sequins

Remove flounce

Alternate layers of pink and orange fringe up to the bustline; glue orange sequins to cover the edge of fringe

Cut off skirt

Dress

3. I made a string purse out of the big bow I cut off the bodice. Glue the cut edge under, tie it up with pink ribbon and glue orange fringe on the bottom.

4. The headpiece is a piece of elasticized sequins hooked together with a pin. Glue feathers on the inside of the pin and a piece of jewelry on the outside. Add beads, a bracelet and a feather boa.

Zoot Suit

Zoot Suit

To accomplish the look of a zoot suit, you must first find a jacket or suit that is too large for the person wearing it. You will want the shoulders of the jacket big enough to add large shoulder pads, and the pants should rise high on the waist and have suspenders.

Making the Costume

1. If you don't have extra-large shoulder pads, you can make them out of foam. Cut out a square. Slit one corner and glue it to itself. Round the rest of it off with scissors. Glue it into the shoulder of the over-sized jacket.

2. I had to glue the sleeves under because they were too long.

3. Originally, I bought a pair of pants to go with the jacket but later decided on a pair of dark pants. I added suspenders.

4. Add a red shirt, wide tie, fedora and a chain that is attached inside the jacket. It should reach to the pocket of the pants and have keys on the end. A big scarf in the pocket finishes off the costume.

5. For spats, I used socks with pieces of elastic under the shoes.

Over-sized Suit

1930s

Thirties Woman

Thirties Woman

When I think of the Thirties, I think of Loretta Young in an evening gown. The dresses always seemed to have that sheer look around the neck and upper chest and a slinky gown. You could see the straps of the gown beneath the sheer fabric. I couldn't find a gown even close to what I was looking for, but I had a wonderful long, black slip, which when added to a sheer nightie gave me the Thirties' look.

Sheer Nightie

Making the Costume

1. Cut the sheer nightie off at the hips. Leave it long enough that it will stay tucked in well.

2. Turn the nightie backwards. Put the long black slip over it. Add long black gloves, beads and a feather boa. The boa is optional.

Slip

Bellboy

If my Thirties woman happens to be staying in a hotel for the evening, she might be helped to her room by a bellboy. He would carry her bags and open the door. His costume was quite specific so that you could find him easily in a group of people. I purchased a dark blue suit for the bellboy.

Making the Costume

1. Jacket: Pull the lapel closed to the neck. Trim the collar off so you end up with a small stand-up collar. Glue gold fabric around the collar and add a fabric paint button in gold glitter.

2. Tack hook-and-loop tape at the neck to hold the jacket closed. You may need to press the lapels out so there is no crease.

Bellboy

3. Using the existing buttons, cover them with gold fabric paint. Let them dry. Lay the jacket out flat with the two buttons buttoned and the hook-and-loop tape fastened. Make gold fabric paint buttons on the front of the jacket.

4. Glue gold trim around where the buttons are located. Cut off the jacket, leaving it longer and in a point at the front. Glue the edge under.

5. Glue gold trim around the cuffs and down the legs of the pants. Add gloves.

6. The hat is made from the bottom of a plastic bottle. I covered it with the leftover fabric from the jacket, added gold trim and fabric paint buttons, and secured it with a chin strap.

Suit

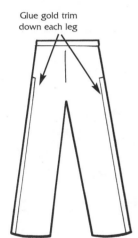

Glue gold trim down each leg

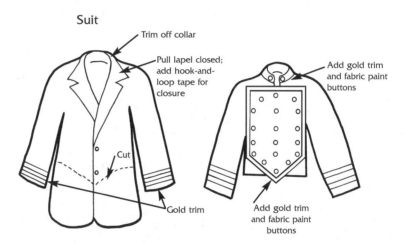

Suit

Trim off collar

Pull lapel closed; add hook-and-loop tape for closure

Cut

Gold trim

Add gold trim and fabric paint buttons

Add gold trim and fabric paint buttons

Cigarette Girl

If my Thirties woman decides to wander into the lounge of the hotel, she might be approached by a cigarette girl. It was permissible back then to smoke everywhere.

Making the Costume

1. Pink dress: Cut the skirt off short. Cut off the netting from under the lower skirt and sew it into the angled waist to make the skirt stand out more. Glue sequin trim around the skirt.

2. Glue alternating red, pink and orange sequin trim to the bodice. I changed the spaghetti straps so they went around the neck like a halter top. Add a pink silk rose to one side of the neckline. Add long red gloves.

Cigarette Girl

Dress

3. The hat is the bottom of a plastic bottle covered with pink fabric cut from the skirt. Glue the fabric to the plastic and cover the edges with sequin trim. Add feathers.

4. Cigarette tray: I used a white cardboard box. Glue the flaps closed. Cut the center out of the top of the box, leaving a lip around it. Glue fringe around the bottom. Glue rows of sequins from the fringe to the top. A piece of pink trim fastens around the back of the neck to hold the tray in place. When you fasten on the strap, be sure you use a pin on each side and cover with sequins. The strap will be sturdier and hold together longer.

5. I glued sequins across the toe of the high heels to finish the look.

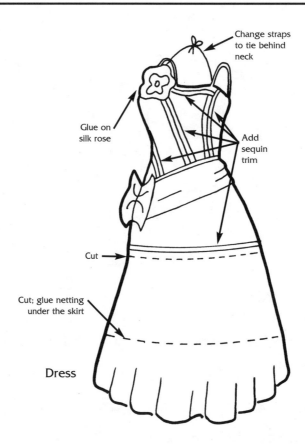

Dress

1940s

Forties Woman

Forties Woman

Forties Woman
Original Dress

Except for the length, I found a great red dress I knew would make a stunning Forties woman with very little work. The only thing necessary was to glue the bottom of an old heavy slip to the hem of the dress. It worked.

I found an old stole at a local rummage sale for three dollars. I added rhinestones at the waist of the dress and on the stole, black gloves and a black felt hat. Doesn't she look like she's ready to step on a train back in time?

World War II Man and Woman

Even though the costumes of this chapter are done easily, I wanted to show you what they looked like. You can find, as I have many times, all manner of military suits at salvage stores and second-hand shops. It is still pretty easy and reasonable to find soldier uniforms from World War II.

To make the woman's black suit, I merely put a jacket over a dress, added trim around the neck of the dress, pearls, white gloves and a black felt hat.

There are many other styles from the period, but I chose this one as the perfect representation of the women of the day.

**World War II
Man and Woman**

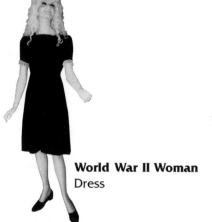

World War II Woman
Dress

World War II Woman
Jacket

1950s

Beatnik Man

Beatnik Man

Every period had its rebels. One of the off-beat groups of the Fifties was the beatniks. They hung out in coffee shops, smoked strong cigarettes in cigarette holders, and recited poetry while snapping their fingers. As a rule, they dwelled on the darker side of life.

The tendency in dress was toward dark colors. I purchased a black crew-neck shirt and a pair of black slacks as a starting point. All I had to do next was buy accessories.

The scarf, vest, beret and sunglasses all came from a local thrift shop. For cigarette holders, see the resource section at the back of the book.

Beatnik Woman

The female counterpart for the beatnik man was similarly dressed. I located a pair of stirrup pants and cut the stirrups off the hem of the legs. Next I found a black turtleneck and a long vest. With the addition of the necklace, beret, sunglasses and long cigarette holder, the beatnik woman was complete. She can also be done with black tights and a short dark skirt. The main thing is to keep the basic garments dark colored and add accessories.

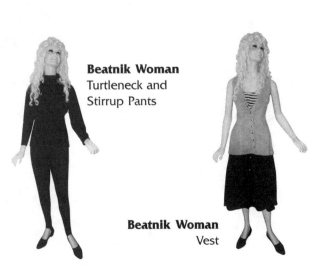

Beatnik Woman
Turtleneck and
Stirrup Pants

Beatnik Woman
Vest

Beatnik Woman

Fifties Woman

Fifties Woman

If you didn't happen to be in one of the more rebellious groups and were still in high school or college, as a young woman you might wear a mid-length skirt, blouse, stretchy belt and scarf around the neck.

I started out with a pink mid-length skirt and a white, frilly blouse, but changed my mind on the blouse and bought another to finish out the costume. It is a pretty simple look but works for the period.

Fifties Man

I couldn't believe my eyes, when I walked into a thrift shop and saw the man's shirt. Even though it was made recently, it looked like the short-tailed, jacket-style shirts from the Fifties. I purchased a pair of dark gray pants to complete the costume.

Can't you see the two of them strolling around the campus of a picturesque college quad or at the bowling alley with friends?

Fifties Man

Fifties Poodle Skirt Girl

The garments for the Fifties Poodle Skirt Girl are quite easy to find in thrift shops. Adding a poodle to the skirt is optional. You can make them with pieces of fake fur and fabric paint. Since the skirt I chose was a thin fabric, I chose not to do a poodle. Most of the poodle skirts were made of felt.

See the section on underskirting or the resource section in the back of the book for places to purchase underskirting.

The shoes were quite simple. Using a pair of cheap white canvas tennis shoes, I glued black fabric to the tops of the shoes and covered the edges with black fabric paint. This gives you the look of the 1950s saddle shoe cheaply, with very little work.

Fifties Girl

1960s

Hippie Man

I like to do the rebellious groups from the periods, because, for one thing, they dressed dramatically so they would be noticed as different. For myself, I thought the flower children were certainly an interesting bunch. They were against everything in government, including war. It seemed that they just wanted to smoke their dope and make love. If you were to wander into a commune back then, you might see a man dressed like my hippie man.

Hippie Man

Making the Costume

1. Striped jeans: I bought a second pair of dark blue jeans, cut a large vee out of each leg and glued it into a slit cut from the hem of the striped jeans to below the knee. The hippie man wore wide bell bottoms that touched the ground.

2. I found a zipper-front, brown pullover shirt and white belt, but it was still missing something. The vest was from an old suit I used for another costume. By cutting up a suede cloth skirt, I glued sections on the inside bottom of the vest and fringed it. I added a strip of suede around the center.

3. Add long hair, little round glasses, beads, a hat and sandals, and you have your hippie man.

Hippie Man
Striped Jeans

Hippie Woman

I bought a pair of gaudy flowered, full-legged pants and a black blouse with handkerchief hem sleeves at a rummage sale. It was simple enough to turn the pants inside out and sew in a new seam to make them bell-bottoms. I left out the hem of the blouse and added a belt, beads, hat and flowers in the hair.

Hippie Woman

Hippie Woman
Blouse and Pants

1970s

Rock 'n' Roll Singer

Rock 'n' Roll Singer

To show you how a music legend might dress, I found a woman's large jumpsuit, an old dress with glitz and was on my way.

Making the Costume

1. Cut the dress off just below the waist. The white taffeta underskirting will be used for the cape and the flare in the hems of the pants.

2. Jumpsuit: Cut the legs from the hem to below the knee. Glue or sew a triangle of white taffeta inside the slits to give it that belled look. Trim with white sequins. Cut slits in the sleeves to about four inches above the hem. Glue or sew triangles of material from the dress bodice inside the slits to loosen the sleeves some. Trim with white sequins.

3. Open the neck of the garment to the waist and pull up the collar. By cutting out sections of the dress bodice and gluing it on as shown in the diagram, you will have plenty of sequined glitz without having to sew on one sequin. Glue white fringe down the arms and across the shoulders in back.

4. The belt is a white belt with fabric glued on and the closure in the back under the short cape. I made the big buckle by covering a piece of foam with sequined fabric. The chains give the costume that rock star look. Add sunglasses and gold chains around the neck. The wig has built-in sideburns. See the resource section for the wig.

Dress

Jumpsuit

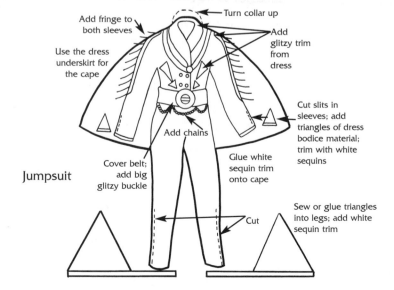

Jumpsuit

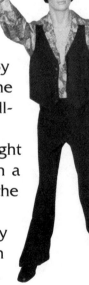

I know that many of these costumes for the 1970s are simple, but they will give you an idea of what people wore during the period and how to make them easily and cheaply from everyday clothing bought at rummage sales or thrift shops.

Seventies Woman

This particular costume is so simple it needs very little explanation. I found a beige woman's suit. It was made of a light-weight, non-fray, suede fabric. I cut off the hem to make a mini-skirt, added a pair of go-go boots, a hat, sunglasses and a necklace, then stepped back in time to the 1970s.

Seventies Woman

Seventies Woman
Suit

Disco Man

The discos were hot with music, dancing and mirrored disco balls and strobe lights highlighted the dance floors. Men were wearing paisley shirts, bell-bottomed pants, vests and gold chains around their necks.

I purchased two pairs of navy blue pants, very close in color. By cutting a triangle out of the outer legs of one pair and splitting the legs of the other, I could sew in the triangle to give the pants that bell-bottom look.

Paisley shirts aren't as easy to find as you might imagine. I ended up buying a woman's silky blouse in a large size. You must leave the shirt open to show the chest and gold chains.

The odd suit vests are easy to find in thrift shops. By adding the vest, a pair of sunglasses and a wig with sideburns, I accomplished the disco man. Men and women were also wearing Afro hairstyles at the time.

Disco Man

Disco Man
Paisley Shirt

1980s

Punk Man

Punk Man
Snakeskin Vest

Punk Man

Punk was the flashy, colorful and strange look of the Eighties rebel. The men tended toward leathers, chains, tattoos and piercings. The hairstyles were the most bizarre yet. Whoopi Goldberg said it best in the movie *Jumpin' Jack Flash* when she saw a punk couple walking down the street and compared them to a tropical fish and its mate. I loved that.

Although many of the people who dressed in the punk style spiked their hair and colored it brightly, I decided to go with normal hair colors in the punk style.

When I found a snakeskin vest at a local yard sale, I knew it wouldn't take much to make the punk man. I used a pair of black jeans and bought accessories at a junk store. The bracelets are made from a black belt fastened with hook-and-loop tape. I took apart an old necklace for the chains attached to the bracelets. The belt is leather with fabric paint drops to make it look studded. Chain necklaces, an earring and colored sunglasses gave him the look I wanted.

The boots are spray painted on the bottom; the top was already a pinky red color. I merely added more chains. For the wig, see the resource section at the back of the book.

Punk Woman

I dyed a short polka-dotted jacket so the dots turned pink and glued the sleeves from an old wedding dress into the short sleeves of the jacket. The can-can was purchased at a thrift shop. I cut the waist off to make it shorter and put in new elastic. By putting both pieces over a short black slip and adding black fishnet hose, socks and boot shoes, I knew I was almost there. A studded belt, jewelry and a wig finished the costume.

Punk Woman
Slip

Punk Woman
Jacket

Punk Woman

Summary

Costumes from the different periods are as diverse as the people who wore them. I have shown you but a few examples of each period as I interpreted them.

Through my examples, I hope I have given you enough ideas that you will be able to find pictures of what you want for a period costume and will be able to figure out in a simple, cheap way how to accomplish the look.

Most of the costumes in this book are now the property of Broadway Bazaar Costumes in Mattoon, Illinois, and are being used for rentals.

Anything in this book not purchased second-hand can be found through the resource section at the back of the book.

The next time you are involved in a costume party, a play, a parade or a dress-up night at a convention, I hope you will think of this book and have the fun and satisfaction of making your own costume. If you follow my guide, you should be the hit of the event.

Resources

Caufield's Novelties
1006 W. Main St.
Louisville, KY 40202
1-800-777-5653

Costumes, Accessories

Eddie's Trick Shop
262 Rio Circle
Decatur, GA 30030
(404) 377-0003
1-800-404-0003

Makeup, clown supplies,
wigs, masks, costumes,
props

Hatcrafters, Inc.
20 N. Springfield Rd.
Clifton Heights, PA 19018
(610) 623-2620

Custom-made costume,
uniform, and military
reproduction head wear

Junk for Joy
3314 W. Magnolia Blvd.
Burbank, CA 91505
(818) 569-4903

Vintage clothes, shoes,
hats, costume
accessories

Lacey Costume Wigs
505 8th Ave. 11th Floor
New York, NY 10018
(212) 695-1996
1-800-562-9911
Fax (212) 695-3860

Historial costume,
character and theatrical
wigs and hair pieces

Magique Novelties
240 South Westgate Drive
Carol Stream, IL 60188
(630) 653-7712

Costume accessories,
props and novelties

Masters Treasures
Masters Tuxedos
3600 Market St.
Youngstown, OH 44507
(330) 788-9932
1-800-321-0087

Men's vintage formal wear, including all varieties of suits, tuxedos, ties, shirts, etc., as well as made-to-order

Morris Costumes
4300 Monroe Rd.
Charlotte, NC 28205
(704) 333-4653
1-800-334-4678

Costumes, accessories, masks, props

Oriental Trading
4206 S. 108th St.
Omaha, NE 68137
1-800-228-0475

Mail-order catalog for costume accessories

Red Hill Adhesives
1540 Biglerville Road
Gettysburg, PA 17325
(717) 337-3038
1-800-822-4003

Suppliers of glue guns and glue

Rubie's Costume Company
12008 Jamaica Ave.
Jamaica, NY 11418
(718) 846-1008

Costumes, accessories, makeup, wigs

Sculptural Arts Coating, Inc.
501 Guilford Ave.
Greensboro, NC 27401
(336) 379-7651
1-800-743-0379
www.sculpturalarts.com

Artists' choice Saturated Paints ™ and Sculptor Coat®— used for making masks, costumes, hats, jewelry and make-up special effects

Sweetheart Slips
14837 N.E. 20th Ave.
N. Miami, FL 33181
(305) 919-7737
1-800-227-7547
Fax (305) 919-9566

Zucker Feather Products
512 N. East St., Box 331
California, MO 65018
(573)796-2183

All types of women's
slips

Feathers and feather trim

About the Author

A single mother for many years, Barb Rogers haunted thrift shops, rummage sales and auctions in the hope of finding old clothes that could be converted into costumes and sold. Not a seamstress, unable to use a pattern and without a sewing machine, she developed her own unique way of designing costumes.

After returning to school, she completed a Bachelor's Degree from Eastern Illinois University, where she studied psychology and communications, but her first love remained costuming.

Broadway Bazaar Costumes was born in one upstairs room, on the main street of Mattoon, Illinois, with 130 costumes, and Barb's burning desire to succeed. Within five years, it had grown to fifteen rooms of fun, fabulous, flamboyant costumes.

A member of the National Costumers Association, Barb attended national conventions, competed with costumers from all over the U.S. and won many awards. But after ten years in business, she was brought down by a serious illness.

Always the survivor and eternal optimist, but unable to continue running the shop, she leased it out and found her second love: writing. Barb, her husband Junior, and their two dogs, Sammi and Georgie, relocated to a small mountain community in Arizona, where she could heal and write. Since that time, in addition to working on her costuming books, Barb has written a murder mystery, two romance novels and two inspirational novels.

At age fifty-one, Barb hopes to become a published novelist but will always hold on to costuming as her first love.

Order Form

Meriwether Publishing Ltd.
PO Box 7710
Colorado Springs CO 80933-7710
Phone: 800-937-5297 Fax: 719-594-9916
Website: www.meriwether.com

Please send me the following books:

_____ **Instant Period Costumes #BK-B244** $19.95
by Barb Rogers
How to make classic costumes from cast-off clothing

_____ **Costuming Made Easy #BK-B229** $19.95
by Barb Rogers
How to make theatrical costumes from cast-off clothing

_____ **Elegantly Frugal Costumes #BK-B125** $14.95
by Shirley Dearing
A do-it-yourself costume maker's guide

_____ **Broadway Costumes on a Budget #BK-B166** $15.95
by Janet Litherland and sue McAnally
Big-time ideas for amateur producers

_____ **Costuming the Christmas and Easter Play** $12.95
#BK-B180
by Alice M. Staeheli
How to costume any religious play

_____ **Self-Supporting Scenery #BK-B105** $15.95
by James Hull Miller
A scenic workbook for the open stage

_____ **Stage Lighting in the Boondocks #BK-B141** $12.95
by James Hull Miller
A simplified guide to stage lighting

These and other fine Meriwether Publishing books are available at your local bookstore or direct from the publisher. Prices subject to change without notice. Check our website or call for current prices.

Name: _____

Organization name: _____

Address: _____

City: _____ State: _____

Zip: _____ Phone: _____

❑ **Check enclosed**
❑ **Visa / MasterCard / Discover #** _____

Expiration
Signature: _____ *date:* _____
   (required for credit card orders)

Colorado residents: Please add 3% sales tax.
Shipping: Include $3.75 for the first book and 75¢ for each additional book ordered.

❑ *Please send me a copy of your complete catalog of books and plays.*